Classical World Series

THE ROMAN SATIRISTS AND THEIR MASKS

Susanna Morton Braund

D1637585

Bristol Classical Press

General Editor: John H. Betts
Series Editor: Michael Gunningham

Cover illustration: Roman portrait busts
(drawn by Christine Hall)

First published in 1996 by
Bristol Classical Press
an imprint of
Gerald Duckworth & Co. Ltd
61 Frith Street
London W1V 5TA

Reprinted 1999

A CIP catalogue record for this book
is available from the British Library

ISBN 1-85399-139-2

Available in USA and Canada from:
Focus Information Group
PO Box 369
Newburyport
MA 01950

Printed and bound in Great Britain by
Antony Rowe Limited

Contents

Preface

This is positively the last general book on Roman satire I shall write. (There's a hostage to fortune!) Let me say a few words about how it came to be written. The editor of the series, Michael Gunningham, invited me to write it more years ago than I care to admit. But it has been a long time coming and I am grateful to the Press for not pulling the plug on it. The book has been in my head since I first drafted the proposal for the Press, yet most of it was written during my long-awaited study leave in the Spring of 1995. I hope it is worth waiting for.

In the end I enjoyed writing it very much, but it was not an easy book to write. One of my key aims was to produce something entirely complementary to the overview I offered in *Roman Verse Satire*, which appeared in 1992 in the Greece & Rome survey series, *New Surveys in the Classics* (no. 23). In *The Roman Satirists and their Masks* I have tried to find a radically different approach to the subject of Roman satire. Because of my increasing interest in viewing literature as performance and because of my conviction that the creation of different characters or 'masks' – a result of the Greek and Roman training in rhetoric – is central to any understanding of Latin literature, I decided to treat the texts of Roman satire as performances and to consider the characters whose voices we hear in these performances. To this extent, the book can be seen as the culmination of my work on *persona* theory in Roman satire. And I hope that my act of cutting up the subject and pasting it together in a way not done before will stimulate debate and reaction by shaking people out of assumptions that they may never have questioned. Above all, I hope that it will provide an accessible way into the fascinating genre of Roman satire for students meeting it for the first time.

Only a fool would offer a typescript like this to the Press without testing it against the 'critical nail' (Persius *Satire* 1.65) first. The willing guinea-pigs were my friends Barbara Bell and Jonathan Walters. Both have improved the book immeasurably and I am most grateful to them. In particular, the addition of the glossary of technical terms (with the terms listed marked * on their first occurrence) was Barbara's suggestion. I am grateful too to the editor of the series, Michael Gunningham, for his careful attention to detail and to John Betts, as my colleague at Bristol and as 'Mr Bristol Classical Press' for his continued support and advice. I am delighted to be able to use the excellent translation of Juvenal by Niall Rudd, for the excerpts quoted. These are reproduced by the kind permission of Oxford University Press (N. Rudd, *Juvenal. The Satires*, Oxford World's Classics series, 1992). The quotations from Lucilius are reprinted by permission of the publishers of the Loeb Classical Library from *Remains of Old Latin vol. 3*, translated by E.H. Warmington, Cambridge, Mass., Harvard University Press, (1938 repr. 1979). The translations of Horace and Persius are my own. The photograph of Stephen Fry as Juvenal (from the programme on Juvenal entitled *Laughter and Loathing*, BBC2, August 1995) was supplied by the BBC Picture Archives. The three drawings within the text are original line drawings taken from the 1831 edition by A.J. Valpy of Theophrastus' Characters. The engraving used to illustrate the angry satirist is 'The Morose', the mocking satirist is 'The Dissembler' and the smiling satirist is 'The Plausible'. I am grateful to John Betts for drawing my attention to them. Finally, the fine cover drawings (after Roman portrait busts) are by Chris Hall: to her, my profound thanks.

This was a project which was often elusive and sometimes downright stubborn. It resisted being written. The greatest encouragement to bring it into realisation came from Adam Morton – and to him above all I am grateful.

Introduction to Roman Satire: The Basics

Old and new ways into Roman satire

Studying ancient literature is like detective work. We have to piece together the evidence which survives from antiquity and make intelligent guesses about what does not survive. This is especially true of Roman satire, where there are authors whose work survives only in fragments or not at all. The detective work does not end there. To make intelligent guesses about Roman satire we have to try to shed our modern prejudices about literature, modern prejudices which we are often hardly aware of, modern prejudices which can easily blur our view of ancient literature. Important questions to ask include: Who writes literature? From what social and educational background? Why? For what audience? What did 'publication' consist of? What are the shared expectations of author and audience? The last of these questions is the largest and in this book I shall attempt to suggest some fruitful approaches.

Some of the questions posed here can be answered with reference to Roman literature in general. Roman literature was the almost exclusive preserve of a tiny élite of wealthy, highly-educated men of well-born and well-connected families. Such men divided their time between 'business' (*negotium*) – primarily politics, in the widest sense of competing for power and status and other rewards – and leisure (*otium*). Their education in literature and rhetoric was designed to equip them for both of these aspects of their adult lives. Not that these are watertight categories. The leisure activity of 'literature' can function in the political realm, just as politics can surface within literature and can shape it. This is evident, for example, in the occasion of the literary recitation, which (at least from the time of Horace onwards) was a prime way of disseminating new literary works. Whether a private recitation at a dinner-party attended by 'friends' (i.e. patrons and clients) or a more formal public occasion, the recitation displayed and reinforced the power relationships at the heart of Roman society. Recitations were a part of the structure of 'friendship' (*amicitia*) at which debts and obligations between individuals were advertised or created. For example, a powerful person, a 'patron' might hold a recitation of his own poetry which his friends of inferior status, his 'clients', had to attend. Or a patron might host a recitation at which one of his clients who wrote poetry was able to present his works, to

which the patron's other clients and maybe his patrons too, more powerful men again, would be invited. The patron in turn would support his
powerful friends by attending any recitations which they hosted. It is
important to bear in mind that for the Romans 'literature' is always
situated within the context of 'friendship' (*amicitia*). This emerges
particularly so in the case of Roman satire, in which friendship is a
prominent theme.

The social context of literature will be a concern throughout this
book. To provide a basis for my interpretation of satire, I use the
introduction to this book to provide a brief outline of the genre* of
Roman verse satire, starting with its origins and sketching its development through more than three centuries. This traditional type of literary
history can, of course, be found in and supplemented from other textbooks. My aim here is to introduce the reader to the authors of Roman
verse satire and the extent and scope of their work before I move to an
approach which emphasises not the authors but what they created.

The seven chapters of the book itself will attempt a fresh approach
to Roman verse satire. Instead of chapters arranged in chronological
sequence devoted to each satirical poet in turn, the central approach of
this volume will be to treat satire as drama, on the basis that the authors
of satire are not engaged in autobiography but use masks (*personae*) in
their satire, a theory which is illuminated by the broader context of the
Roman rhetorical training shared by author and audience (ch.1). The
three chapters which follow will examine the three most prominent
masks created by the satirical poets: the angry character (ch.2); the
laughing, mocking character (ch.3); and the smiling, ironic character
(ch.4). In these three chapters I shall draw substantial amounts of
illustrative material from the best-known satires, primarily of Horace and
Juvenal. An important feature will be my use of the term 'the satirist' to
denote not the author but the character created (as I shall explain in
chapter 1).

In chapter 5 I shall analyse the relationship between the satirist
and society by considering the imagery used of satirists by themselves
and by others: does he belong in society or is he essentially an outsider?
Then, using an analogy with cinema, I shall investigate the authority of
the satirist, which makes satire seem at times so realistic (ch. 6). Developing the argument of chapter 1, I shall underline how the rhetorical
background shapes satire and I shall show how satire's relationship with
epic is another important influence. After this demonstration of the
'literariness' and sophistication of Roman satire, which makes it hard to
use as source material on Roman society, I shall close this chapter by

suggesting ways in which Roman satire can be used as evidence for Roman life. In the final chapter (ch. 7) I shall consider the relationship between satirists and their audiences, inside and outside of the text. The genre of satire, which calls itself 'conversation' (*sermo*), uses a variety of forms – monologue, dialogue and letter – which subtly affect the relationships between the different voices and listeners. My analysis will highlight the wide range of potential relationships between author and audience in this genre which is a significant factor in making satire tricky and slippery to interpret. Satire, after all, provokes perhaps the strongest emotions and the widest range of reactions in its audience. This prompts the question whether or not there is, or can ever be, a 'right' response to it. My view is that of course there are better- and worse-informed readings of satire, but that, ultimately, any individual's response is inevitably a product of the way they interact with that particular text. Because satire engages so closely with its readers, the potential for attraction to and repulsion from the character of the satirist and the views he (usually he, not she) expresses is enormous. That is what generates such a variety of responses.

Suggestions for further study and further reading follow and a glossary of technical terms (marked in the text by * the first time each occurs) and an index of the poems discussed conclude the volume.

Roman satire – truly Roman

The origins of Roman verse satire are obscure, although various theories are offered by the Romans themselves. What seems clear is that there is no Greek original on which the writers of Roman satire modelled their works. That's how Horace can describe satire as a Roman genre, 'verse never handled by the Greeks' (*Satires* 1.10.66) and the first century AD professor Quintilian can claim Roman supremacy in this genre: 'Satire is entirely our own' (*The Training of an Orator, Institutio Oratoria* 10.1.93). Ancient theories connect the name *satura* with ideas of variety and abundance. Most appealing is the explanation which makes the author of satire a cook serving up to his audience a sausage stuffed full of varied ingredients. Other theories offer possible links with drama. The combination of humour and mockery suggested a link between *satura* and satyrs, presumably as portrayed in satyr plays, the obscene after-pieces to Greek tragedies, and the satirical poets themselves claim Greek Old Comedy as an ancestor (Hor. *Sat.* 1.4.1-5, 1.10.16, Pers. 1.123-4). Livy goes further than this and includes in his account of the development of Roman drama a musical stageshow without an organised plot which he names *satura* (7.2.4-10). Such ideas, although not necessarily to be accepted literally, are valuable for their emphasis upon the dramatic dimension in satire.

The earliest known proponent of the genre was Ennius (239-169 BC), who was from the south of Italy and therefore influenced by the cultures of Greece, southern Italy and Rome. Perhaps it was this multiculturalism which inspired his many literary innovations. He is most famous for his establishment of Latin epic in his *Annales* (*Annals*). But his literary experiments were not confined to epic: he also wrote various types of drama and four books of *Saturae*. Unfortunately, only 31 lines of his satires survive. But even from these few fragments we can see that the poems were in a variety of metres and on a variety of themes – a real miscellany, fitting with the ancient explanations which connect *satura* with ideas of variety and abundance.

Lucilius – a father figure for the genre

Ennius' satires were clearly experimental. That is perhaps why it was not Ennius but Lucilius who was regarded by later writers of satire as the founder of the genre (e.g. Hor. *Sat.* 1.10.48). Gaius Lucilius (died 102/1 BC, an old man) was a wealthy aristocrat (*eques*) from Campania and member of the politically powerful and culturally influential clique around Scipio Aemilianus, the general, politician and patron of the arts. Lucilius wrote thirty books of satires, initially continuing Ennius' experiments with metre but then settling upon the hexameter* of epic and so standardising the metre of the genre. Only 1300 fragments survive of his thirty books and of these the longest is only 13 lines long. This makes it hard to reconstruct his satires with confidence. But features which later appear as standard were established by Lucilius. These include use of the first person ('autobiographical') presentation and the loose construction suited to 'conversations' (*sermones*); the range of subject-matter including criticism of morality in public and private life and criticism of literature and language; and the range of language available in satire, from mundane and obscene words, usually excluded from poetry, through technical vocabulary, to grand words of the epic register and epic quotation and parody. It is also clear that Lucilius used his satires to stage vigorous political attacks upon some of Scipio's enemies, for example, the Lupus and Mucius mentioned by Persius in his *Satire* 1.115 (see p. 40 below). More generally, he presents an assertive view of political morality, for example, in the so-called *Virtus* fragment (1196-1208W), making his satires reflect the ideals and aspirations of Scipio's clique (see Hor. *Sat.* 2.1.62-74).

Horace – a new Lucilius for the Augustan age

The next satirical poet known to us is Horace, writing at least 70 years later. Quintus Horatius Flaccus (65-8 BC) refers to Lucilius in a mixture of praise and criticism to establish his own literary, moral and political credentials as his successor – a new Lucilius for a new age. According to Horace, Maecenas and Octavian are the focus of culture and power, as Scipio was for Lucilius. In contrast with Lucilius, Horace's social position was not one of security and independence. His father was a freedman who made a fortune from his activities an as entrepreneur and who lavished money on giving his son an education fit for a young man of higher social standing. With this good start in life, Horace at the age of 21 became attached to the staff of Brutus and the following year was appointed tribune of the soldiers, thereby gaining equestrian status. But disaster then struck: in 42 BC Brutus committed suicide after his defeat by Antony at the battle of Philippi and on his return home Horace found himself in difficult economic circumstances. He was then fortunate and shrewd enough to find a permanent position in the public finance office and in 38 BC was introduced by his friend Virgil to Maecenas, a rich and influential patron, and later to Octavian, the future emperor Augustus. Horace soon produced his first publication, *Satires* Book 1, in 35-4 BC. After the battle of Actium in 31 BC he published the second Book of *Satires* and the *Epodes*. *Odes* 1-3 were published together in 23 BC. He returned to the form of hexameter satire in *Epistles* 1, published in 20-19 BC, and in *Epistles* 2.2 which appeared the following year. He resumed lyric in 17 BC with the *Secular Hymn* (*Carmen Saeculare*), commissioned by Augustus for the Secular Games and in 13 BC with the publication of *Odes* 4. It is hard to date *Epistles* 1 and the so-called *Art of Poetry* (*Ars Poetica*). Throughout his work Horace articulates the ideology* of the élite group of which he was a member.

Persius' concentrated brew

After Horace, the next exponent of satire whose work survives is the Neronian poet Persius. Aules (possibly Aulus) Persius Flaccus (AD 34-62) was born in Etruria into an important family of high status and educated at Rome as a pupil of Cornutus the Stoic. He took no part in public life but seems to have moved in elevated circles and was acquainted with the epic poet Lucan, who greatly admired his single book of *Satires*. This brief book of less than seven hundred lines, which may or may not be complete, consists of six satires preceded by a prologue. They are packed with literary echoes and allusions, showing in particular an intimate familiarity with the satirical works of Lucilius and Horace. Yet at the same time they are entirely original, thanks to Persius' self-presentation as an angry and alienated young man (see discussion of the *persona* below).

Of the satirical poets writing in Quintilian's time, the 'eminent satirists today who will be celebrated in the future' (*Institutio Oratoria* 10.1.94), nothing survives beyond the name of one, Turnus, writing under Domitian. We can only guess at the kind of influence he and the others may have exercised upon Juvenal.

The grand rhetoric of Juvenal

Little is known about the life and circumstances of Juvenal (Decimus Iunius Iuuenalis). He is described as eloquent by his contemporary Martial and his satires reflect the rhetorical training received by the Roman élite; the fact that his satires are not dedicated to any patron may indicate that he was of relatively high social status, like Lucilius and Persius. His sixteen Satires, of which the last breaks off in a patently unfinished state, were published in five books. Book 1 comprises *Satires* 1-5, Book 2 *Satire* 6 alone, Book 3 *Satires* 7-9, Book 4 *Satires* 10-12, and Book 5 *Satires* 13-16 (the last poem is unfinished). The few datable references suggest that the first two books were written in the second decade of the second century AD, towards the end of Trajan's reign or, possibly, soon after Hadrian's accession in AD 117. The third book appears to have been written early in Hadrian's reign and the fifth book dates from after AD 127. Juvenal, then, was writing his *Satires* at about the same time as Tacitus was writing his *Annals*, which strike the modern reader as so similar in their biting tone.

He is renowned for his angry tone of voice, a tone which he developed from Persius' creation of the angry young man. What is less often appreciated is that Juvenal experimented with satire as he wrote and that he developed his satiric voice from one of anger to one of ironic detachment in the later satires. Throughout, he uses the 'grand style' inspired by rhetoric and epic to set satire on a new level, very different from the lowly 'conversations' of Horace. But it is the vigour and vehemence of Juvenal's savage indignation (*saeva indignatio*) that determined ideas of 'satire' for ever after. The acute cruelty of *Private Eye* and *Spitting Image* owes a great deal to Juvenal.

Chapter 1
The Masks of Satire

Satire as drama

To view satire as a kind of drama is perhaps the most illuminating approach available. There is some basis for this in the ancient evidence about the origins of satire. We have seen in the Introduction that there may be a link between *satura* and satyrs and that Livy's account of the history of Roman drama included a stage-show called *satura* (p.x). Moreover, the satirists themselves connect their work with Greek Old Comedy. But whether or not such links are accepted, the analogy between satire and drama invites thoughts of performance. These are poems written not to be read silently but to be performed in front of an audience. The view of satire as drama reminds us that the authors of satire are using dramatic forms, primarily the monologue and the dialogue. (These and other forms will be discussed in Chapter 7.) This use of the forms of drama distinguishes satire from epic (whose hexameter metre it borrows), in which the predominant form is third person narrative. (For the relation between satire and epic see Chapter 6.) Satire, then, combines the forms of drama with the metre of epic. It is a hybrid form.

To view satire as a kind of drama, as a performance, helps us resist seeing satire as autobiography. This type of interpretation, which was prominent earlier this century, is the result of a post-Romantic* view of poetry as the expression of emotions straight from the heart. The fact that satire often uses the first person presentation doubtless seemed to support such a view. It is now generally accepted that this kind of post-Romantic interpretation is inappropriate to any kind of Roman poetry, even love poetry. Roman poetry is the product of a highly educated élite and an arena in which the intellect as much as the emotions are exercised. To ask if the expressions of the passions of anger or pity or love are what we would call 'genuine' is not a question the Romans would have framed or even, perhaps, understood. For the Romans, the most important ideas were those of plausibility (*fides*) and appropriateness (*decorum*): how *convincing* a display of anger or pity or love is this? This throws the emphasis onto the quality of the performance. That is why it is helpful to see satire as a type of drama. And that is why I distinguish between

1

the authors of satire and the 'satirists' they create in their poems: these dramatic characters who perform upon the satiric stage are not to be confused with the writers of satire.

Masks and satire

To see satire as a type of drama leads easily to the idea that the writers of satire use various masks or *personae* in their poems. Many types of theatrical performance in Greco-Roman antiquity used masks (*personae*) which served as an instant kind of characterisation. This was especially so where there were stock characters with stock masks. For example, in 'New Comedy' written in Athens by Menander and others in the fourth century BC and imitated in Rome by Plautus and Terence in the early second century BC, the irritable old father and his son, the love-lorn young man, the domineering old wife and the scheming slave are some of the stock characters. And in the native Italian form of drama called the Atellan farce stock characters included the fool and the glutton. Rather like the dramatic poets, the writers of Roman satire are creating roles, even if those roles are complex and ambiguous and, at times, shifting. And this view of the voices of Roman satire as a series of *personae* would not have been alien or difficult for the original Roman audiences. It seems that the Romans thought of life, perhaps more than we do, in terms of roles performed and the variety of *personae* adopted in differing circumstances.

A very explicit statement of this outlook is found in Cicero's theory in *On Duties* (*De officiis*) 1 concerning the four *personae* available to each individual. The first *persona* is the universal one of the human self, of being a human as opposed to an animal; the second *persona* is that of the individual with particular skills and capacities, for example, strength, attractiveness, wit and shrewdness. The third *persona* is that which arises from circumstances, for example, high and low birth, wealth and poverty, and the fourth is the *persona* which consists of our individual choice of role in life. Cicero explains that this might be a decision to specialise in philosophy or law or oratory, to follow in your father's footsteps or deliberately to take a different course. These ideas drawn from Cicero's philosophical analysis of the individual's place in society suggest how readily the Romans thought in terms of *persona* – the image presented to society. And although we do not so readily conceive of ourselves as playing out roles, we might usefully compare the function of 'image-makers' in affecting the popular perception of public figures such as politicians and members of the Royal family, of sporting heroes and film-stars.

The use of the mask to create an image (*persona*) and the emphasis upon plausibility and appropriateness and performance is by no means confined to Roman satire but is part of a much wider phenomenon. It pervaded all aspects of the public life of the Roman élite. Nowhere is this more visible than in the rhetorical education of the young Roman. This education was designed to equip the sons of the élite for life in a highly competitive socio-political milieu in which the chief means of attaining superiority was skill in public speaking. Skill in public speaking centred upon being convincing: acting out the appropriate role in the most effective way possible. For the Romans, drama and rhetoric were mutually interdependent.

Drama and rhetoric

The basic education of young Roman boys from wealthy families was in Latin and Greek language. Then, at about the age of eleven, boys went to the *grammaticus*, the teacher of literature, for lessons in reading and the interpretation of texts. We can get some idea of the syllabus – or at least the ideal syllabus – from Quintilian, a professor who was writing at the end of the first century AD. He laid down the texts that he thought should form the programme of studies for school-boys in his twelve-book *The Training of an Orator* (*Institutio Oratoria*), for example, 1.8.5-6:

> That, then, is an excellent procedure, to begin by reading Homer
> and Virgil, although for the full appreciation of their merits the
> intellect needs to be more firmly developed: but there is plenty
> of time for that, because the boy will read them more than once.
> In the meantime let his mind rise with the sublimity of heroic
> poetry, take its inspiration from the greatness of its theme and
> be filled with the highest feelings. The reading of tragedy is also
> useful, and lyric poets nurture the mind, so long as there is a
> careful selection of not only the authors but also the passages
> from their works which are to be read. For the Greek lyric poets
> are often risqué and even in Horace there are passages which I
> should be unwilling to explain to a class.

Not exactly a Roman National Curriculum, but perhaps the nearest thing! Literature was studied not for its own sake but to develop skill in public speaking. And the most privileged boys, between the ages of fifteen and eighteen usually, proceeded to a teacher who specialised in this type of training – the teacher of rhetoric, the *rhetor*.

The education in rhetoric was modelled on the Greek system in which public speaking was divided into three types of oratory: judicial oratory, deliberative oratory and epideictic oratory. Judicial oratory, also called forensic oratory, consisted of speeches of prosecution and defence in cases being heard in the courts. (The word 'forensic' actually derives from the Roman practice of having its law-courts meet in the forum.) Deliberative oratory involved making speeches advising or urging or rejecting a proposed course of action in the Senate, for example, or any other body making such decisions. And epideictic oratory, that is 'display' oratory, consisted chiefly of speeches of praise (also called panegyrical and encomiastic speeches) about a god or an individual or a city or about a public building such as a temple. The opposite to panegyric is invective, where the 'display' speech attacks an individual or place.

The training in all three kinds of public speaking was done through a combination of exercises and the study of specimen speeches. Students had to compose practice cases on specific or general themes. The earliest Roman handbook which survives, the *Rhetorica ad Herennium*, which dates from around 80 BC, shows the set topics which were thought likely to crop up in senatorial debates and in the law-courts. But our fullest source is the writings of the Elder Seneca of the first half of the first century AD. Seneca's works are memoirs of famous rhetorical teachers and famous orators of his time. This body of Roman declamation*, i.e. public speaking, is divided into *Suasoriae* (persuasions) and *Controversiae* (disputes).

Suasoriae consist of advice given to famous characters from history or legend on the proper course of action they should take. For example, 'Agamemnon deliberates whether to sacrifice Iphigeneia, for Calchas says that otherwise sailing is impossible' (Seneca *Suas.* 3); 'Alexander the Great, warned of danger by an augur, deliberates whether to enter Babylon' (*Suas.* 4); 'Cicero deliberates whether to beg Antony's pardon' (*Suas.* 5); 'Antony promises to spare Cicero's life if he burns his writings: Cicero deliberates whether to do so' (*Suas.* 7). In giving this advice, the orator would often appeal to concepts such as honour (*honestum*), right (*fas*), fairness (*aequum*), advantage (*utile*), obligation (*necessarium*), duty (*pium*) and so on.

In a *controversia*, the speakers argued on opposite sides of a legal or quasi-legal case: competition was, therefore, a central feature of this kind of declamation. Plausibility was important, but so was innovation. These two demands pulled in opposite directions at times, as can be seen from a couple of examples. First, in the case of the prostitute priestess (Seneca *Contr*. 1.2), a virgin who had been captured by pirates and sold into prostitution but later returned to her family seeks a priesthood. The dilemma is deepened by the story: she appealed to her clients for assistance but when one client refused, a struggle followed in which she killed the man; she was, however, acquitted of his murder. The *controversia* consists of arguments as to whether or not the woman is eligible for priestly office, given the legal requirement that a priestess be chaste and pure. Another example is Sen. *Contr*. 1.5, 'The man who raped two girls'. The law cited here is as follows: 'A girl who has been raped may choose either marriage to her ravisher without a dowry or his death.' The situation posed is this: 'On a single night, a man raped two girls. One demands his death, the other marriage.' The *controversia* consists of the arguments for and against the different outcomes. It is a matter of some debate how close such cases were to real-life legal cases. The general suspicion is that the emphasis on originality resulted in a lurid and grotesque flavour which seems to resemble the obsessions of our tabloid newspapers today.

Personae, persuasion and power

The Roman education system, then, was directed towards public speaking. The training in words was paramount: the emphasis was upon anything and everything that might impress and persuade: clever arguments, paradox, point (*sententia*), vivid description (*enargeia**), the arousal of emotions. And this training gave the speaker the means of adopting different *personae* on different occasions, depending on the circumstances, and of doing so convincingly. The young aristocrat needed this skill to succeed, because Roman public and political life centred upon public speaking. Power was in the word. And because this training was shared by the members of the élite, they were in a position to recognise and appreciate the use of precisely this skill by others both in declamation and in other spheres of expression, such as poetry.

Rhetoric and satire: Cicero and Juvenal

An example which brings together rhetorical theory and the practice of Roman satire will show how this works. Cicero provides a list of the topics which an orator can use to arouse indignation or pity from his audience in the conclusion (*peroratio*) of his speech *On Invention (De inventione)* 1.100-9. His extensive list of fifteen topics which can fire the audience's indignation (1.100-5) shows a striking similarity to the kinds of things Juvenal's angry speaker says. It would be possible to draw examples from throughout Satires 1-6 but the point is perhaps made most effectively by focusing upon one extended passage. The closing passage of *Satire* 6 (627-61) is in effect the peroration* to Juvenal's angry satires and it is particularly rich in these marks of indignation. The message here is that women are capable of the worst crimes. This general message corresponds to the following topics in Cicero's list:

> 2. Passionate demonstration of the parties affected by the act which is being denounced: all people or superiors or peers or inferiors.
> 7. Demonstration that the deed was foul, cruel, wicked, tyrannical.

The passage starts with a warning addressed to wards and to children about their stepmothers and mothers :

> Why, now it is lawful to murder a stepson.
> I'm warning orphans as well: if you own a sizeable fortune,
> watch out for your lives; don't trust anything served at table.
> Those blackening cakes are highly spiced with a mother's poison.
> Let somebody else be the first to munch what she who bore you
> offers you; get your nervous tutor to test the drinks.
>
> *(Sat.* 6.628-33)

This corresponds to topic no. 11 in Cicero:

> 11. Demonstration that the crime was committed by a person who least of all should have committed it and who might have been expected to prevent it happening.

The vivid picture created by the details of 631-3 is typical of the graphic descriptions which abound in Juvenal and which put into practice Cicero's advice to the orator:

> 10. Enumeration of the attendant circumstances to make the crime as vivid as possible.

The speaker proceeds to appeal to the Roman state:

> You think this is fiction? That my satire has donned theatrical
>   boots,
> that going beyond the bounds and law of earlier writers
> I am raving in Sophocles' gaping style a lofty song
> of things unknown to Rutulian hills and Latin skies?
>
> (634-7)

This connects with Cicero's first piece of advice to the orator, that
indignation may be aroused by:

> 1. Consideration of the great concern shown by the relevant
>   authority – the gods, ancestors, rulers, states, Senate, authors of
>   laws – about the matter under discussion.

The next lines make it clear that the woman's murder of her children was
premeditated:

> Would it were all a dream. But Pontia cries 'It was me!
> I confess; I got some aconite and administered it to my children.
> The murder was detected and is known to all; but I am the
>   culprit!'
> Two, do you say, at a single meal, you venomous viper,
> two at a sitting? 'Yes, and seven, had there been seven!'
>
> (638-42)

This exactly puts into practice item 6 on Cicero's list:

> 6. Indication that the act was premeditated.

By calling her a 'venomous viper' (641) the speaker places the murderess
on a bestial level, fulfilling another element of Cicero's advice:

> 8. Demonstration that the deed is unique and unknown even
>   among savages, barbarians and wild beasts, typically acts of
>   cruelty committed against parents or children or acts of injustice
>   towards people who cannot defend themselves.

The remainder of the poem introduces a comparison between the horrific
heroines of Greek tragedy and modern women which is designed to show
how much worse modern women are:

> Let us believe what tragedy says concerning Procne
> and the cruel woman of Colchis; I won't dispute it. They too
> dared to commit some monstrous crimes in their generation –
> but not for the sake of cash. Extreme atrocities tend
> to cause less shock when fury incites the female to outrage,
> and when, with their hearts inflamed by madness, they are
>   carried down
> like boulders wrenched from a mountain ridge as the ground
>   collapses
> and the vertical face falls in from beneath the hanging cliff-top.
> I cannot abide the woman who assesses the profit, and coolly
> commits a hideous crime. They watch Alcestis enduring
> death for her man, but if they were offered a similar choice
> they would gladly let their husband die to preserve a lapdog.
> Every morning you meet Eriphyles in dozens, and also
> daughters of Danaus; every street has a Clytemnestra.
> Whereas, however, Tyndareus' daughter wielded an oafish
> and awkward two-headed axe which needed both her hands,
> now the job is done with the tiny lung of a toad -
> though it may need steel if your son of Atreus is now immune,
> as the thrice-defeated monarch was, through Pontic drugs.
>
> (643-61)

This is an excellent case of Cicero's ninth recommendation:

> 9. Comparison of the deed with other crimes to enhance the horror.

And, finally, it is clear that the speaker expects his audience's sympathy throughout, just as the orator trying to simulate and provoke indignation does, according to Cicero:

> 14. Request to the audience to identify with the speaker.

The convergence of rhetorical theory and practice in this passage – and throughout Juvenal's satires – would have been appreciated by his audience who had received the same grounding as the poet. When De Decker entitled his important monograph of 1913 *Juvenalis declamans*, he drew attention to a crucial aspect of Juvenal's approach to satire. This was augmented by Scott's 1927 study of the grand style in Juvenal: anger, after all, is a big emotion and needs an expansive form of expression.

Both scholars understood well the close relationship between Roman poetry and the rhetorical education of the Roman élite. (Modern reservations surrounding the word 'rhetoric' are completely inappropriate in a Roman context. In our society it is possible to say of a politician's speech, 'it's just rhetoric', as a way of dismissing that speech without engaging with it, probably because we feel distanced from the entire process of politics. The élite Romans with whom we are concerned here, by contrast, were constantly engaged in politics.) Juvenal, like his élite audience, was trained to be a showman: to create whatever *persona* is required for the context and to make it a convincing creation. And this does not apply to Juvenal alone. The same applies to whatever *persona* is selected: the mask of anger, the mask of mockery or the mask of irony. In every case, the poems of Roman satire are best understood as performances and as miniature dramas.

Chapter 2
The Angry Satirist

Anger and aggression

Anger, aggression and satire seem to us to go hand in hand. This view is shaped by contemporary political satire and by literary satire of previous centuries such as that of Alexander Pope and Jonathan Swift. Writers of satire such as these were heavily influenced by Roman satire and modelled their vehement attacks on those of Persius and Juvenal in particular. But anger is not the only voice of satire. This chapter commences the analysis of Roman satire with the element in it most easy to relate to. Chapters 3 and 4 will investigate other voices of satire which are less familiar. That's why the focus here will be primarily on Juvenal's angry citizen and on Persius who may be said to have invented the satiric *persona* of the angry young man.

The later writers of Roman satire claim that Lucilius, the founder of the genre, raged angrily against the world (see Hor. *Sat.* 1.10.3-4, 2.1.62-8, Pers. 1.114-15, Juv. 1.165-6). The fragments that survive certainly show that Lucilius made fierce attacks on people, both eminent and lowly, although many of the fragments adopt a conversational tone a long way from anger. Whether or not anger is the predominant mode of Lucilius' satire, it is undoubtedly convenient for the later writers to declare it as such. Horace, because he wants to contrast his modest and moderate style of satire with the ferocity of Lucilius' satire to his own advantage; Persius and Juvenal, because they want to claim Lucilius as a precedent for their (allegedly) fearless attacks upon vice. The satirists claim that their anger is, more specifically, indignation, that is, justified anger. This might be said to validate the loss of self-control by the angry speaker, or at least to make that loss of self-control less culpable, by presenting the indignant satirist as a hero speaking out where others are too afraid to speak. This in turn raises important questions about the relationship between the satirist and society: is he really the champion he claims to be? This complex issue will be explored in Chapter 5. First, I shall focus upon the mask of the angry citizen created by Juvenal.

Juvenal's angry citizen

Probably the most famous portrayal of anger in Roman satire is that in
Juvenal's first *Satire*, which opens with a tirade of angry questions:

> Must I be always a listener only, never hit back,
> although so often assailed by the hoarse *Theseid* of Cordus?
> Never obtain revenge when X has read me his comedies,
> Y his elegies? No revenge when my day has been wasted
> by mighty Telephus or by Orestes who, having covered
> the final margin, extends to the back, and still isn't finished?
>
> (1.1-6)

The strong desire for vengeance here, reminiscent of the stance adopted
by a prosecuting orator, is enhanced by the numerous linguistic signs of
anger: indignant questions, omission of the verb, repetitions, extreme
terms (e.g. 'always' and 'never'), exaggerations and the increasing length
of the questions.

These and other signs of anger – including imagery of fire and
vocabulary relating to enduring ('Why need I tell how my heart shrivels
in the heat of its anger...?' (1.45), 'For who could be so inured / to the
wicked city, so dead to feeling, as to keep his temper / when...?' (1.30-2))
– abound throughout the first two books of Juvenal's *Satires*, in which
he explores the full artistic potential of the voice of indignation. So for
example in *Satire* 3 the character Umbricius delivers a lengthy condemnation of life in Rome which is full of anger:

> I must get away from them and their purple clothes. Shall our
>   friend, here,
> sign before me as a witness and recline above me at dinner –
> one who was blown to Rome by the wind, with figs and damsons?
> Does it count for nothing at all that I, from earliest childhood,
> breathed the Aventine air and was fed on the Sabine berry?
>
> (3.81-5)

And the same goes for the misogynistic speaker of *Satire* 6. Only a few
moments into the poem he is ranting:

> And yet, in a time like ours, you are preparing a contract
> with terms for a binding marriage; by now you're under the
>   comb
> of the senior stylist; perhaps you've placed a ring on her finger.

Postumus marrying? You used to be sane; no doubt about that.
What Fury, then, with her maddening snakes is hunting you
    down?
Can you bear to be the slave of a woman, when so much rope
    is at hand,
when those vertiginous top-floor windows are standing open,
and when the Aemilian bridge nearby offers assistance?
If none of these means of deliverance seems to have any appeal,
don't you think it better to sleep with a little boy-friend?

                                (6.25-34)

And he continues to rant for virtually 700 lines, culminating in the
intensely angry passage discussed above in Chapter 1, which packs in
rhetorical and incredulous questions and exclamations, short sentences
with disrupted rhythm, repetition and apostrophe*, words of rapidly
vacillating levels between the incongruously elevated and the contemp-
tuous, and vocabulary expressing the speaker's inability to endure the
outrages he sees everywhere (651-2).

    The sheer length of the tirades in *Satires* 3 and 6 suggests a lack
of self-control and is therefore another sign of anger. So too is the
apparent lack of structure in these poems. Juvenal has carefully articu-
lated *Satire* 1 to make it resemble the repeated outbursts of an angry man,
whose contemplation of the corruption around him makes him boil over
with rage again and again. His angry exclamations (30, 45, 51-4, 63-4
and 79-80) are presented as climaxes to portrayals of the criminals of
Rome (22-9, 30-44, 46-50, 55-62 and 64-78). At times the angry man
seems to promise discussion of particular topics but shortly afterwards
deviates from that 'programme', apparently carried away by his indignation. E.g.:

The day itself is arranged in a splendid series of highlights:
'The basket', then the city square, with Apollo the lawyer
and the generals' statues – one, which some Egyptian wallah
has had the nerve to set up, listing all his achievements;
pissing (and worse) against his image is wholly in order.
Weary old clients trudge away from the porches, resigning
what they had yearned for, though nothing stays with a man so
    long
as the hope of a dinner. Cabbage and kindling have to be
    purchased.

                                (1.127-34)

This omits most of the day's activities to focus upon the humiliation awaiting the humble client at the end of the day. The departure from the promised topic is a subtle dramatisation of indignation. Similarly in *Satire* 6 there is an apparently programmatic declaration at 474-5 but, instead of detailing the woman's day, the speaker gets drawn into the first item, the way she takes out her grumpiness with her husband on her entire household (475-507). The most blatant example of the angry speaker forgetting where he is and departing from the framework occurs in *Satire* 3, when Umbricius begins addressing the entire body of Roman citizens, as if he were delivering a political speech to a public meeting, instead of enjoying a quiet and private farewell conversation with a friend, which is how the poem is initiated:

> I shan't mince words. My fellow Romans, I cannot put up with
> a city of Greeks; yet how much of the dregs is truly Achaean?
> The Syrian Orontes has long been discharging into the Tiber,
> carrying with it its language and morals and slanting strings,
> complete with piper, not to speak of its native timbrels
> and the girls who are told by their owners to ply their trade at
>   the race-track.
> (That's the place for a foreign whore with a coloured bonnet.)
> Romulus, look – your bumpkin is donning his *Grecian* slippers,
> hanging *Grecian* medals on a neck with a *Grecian* smudge.
> *He*'s from far-off Amydon, *he*'s from Sicyon's heights,
> *these* are from Andros and Samos and Tralles, or else Alabanda.
> They make for the Esquiline, or the willows' hill, intent on
>   becoming
> the vital organs and eventual masters of our leading houses.
> Nimble wits, a reckless nerve, and a ready tongue,
> more glib than Isaeus'. Tell me, what do you think he *is*?
> He has brought us, in his own person, every type you can think of;
> teacher of grammar and speaking, geometer, painter, masseur,
> prophet and tightrope-walker, doctor, wizard – your hungry
> Greekling knows the lot; he'll climb to the sky if you ask him.
>   (3.60-78)

Rebellious anger in Persius

In creating his angry character, Juvenal is developing ideas from Persius. In Persius anger is manifested in many ways. The language used is aggressive, both in the physicalisation of many metaphors and in the compressed and jerky expressions used. Even more striking is the rejection of society and its standards in all spheres of life. Persius presents a stance of scornful isolation immediately, in his prologue to the book, a poem which uses the 'limping iambic'* metre associated with poetry of Greek abuse instead of the hexameter by now standard in satire:

> I didn't cleanse my lips in the nag's spring
> and I didn't dream on two-headed Parnassus,
> as I recall, so as to emerge an instant poet.
> The Heliconians and pale Pirene
> I leave to those who have statues licked
> by hugging ivy; it's as a half-clansman myself
> that I bring our song to the rites of the bards.
>
> (Prologue 1-7)

Persius here rejects the bards' poetic imagery of inspiration with irreverent references to the sacred locations named by poets. Typically he portrays himself as an outsider by describing himself as 'a half-clansman', *semipaganus* (a word typically coined for this occasion), not a full member of the group of bards. Even his choice of a metre other than the hexameter for the prologue marks out his rebellious stance.

This stance of the loner is confirmed in the opening lines of *Satire* 1, where he appears to be quite content with a small or non-existent audience:

> 'O, human neuroses! Life is one huge emptiness!'
> 'Who'll read THAT?' Are you talking to ME? No one, of course.
>   'No one?'
> Perhaps one or two. 'That's a pity and a disgrace.' Why's that?
> Because Polydamas and the Trojan 'dames' prefer Labeo
> to me? Rubbish. If muddled Rome makes light of
> something, don't step in to correct the unfair balance
> in those scales and don't look for anything outside yourself.
> The reason? – At Rome who does not – oh, if I could only rightly
>   say it –
> but I CAN, when I look at our grey hair and at that gloomy life
> of ours and at the things we've been doing since we gave up
>   our marbles,
> since we got the flavour of uncles. Then, then – excuse me
>   (I don't want to,
> I can't help it), but I've a cheeky temper – I cackle.
>
> (1.1-12)

He maintains this stance of isolation throughout the poem by a wholesale rejection of contemporary poetry on the grounds that it is too smooth, weak and artificial. This attack spreads to become a broader attack on the moral spinelessness of contemporary society. This is the essence of the secret which he eventually reveals, after more than a hundred lines which function as justification for the revelation:

> Am I forbidden a mutter? Not even in secret? Not even in a hole?
>   Nowhere?
> I don't care: I'll dig a hole for it here. I have seen it, yes, have
>   seen it for myself, little book:
> who does not have the ears of a donkey? This secret,
> this joke of mine, so insignificant, I'll not sell to you for any
>   *Iliad.*

(1.119-23)

This graphic depiction of intolerance of contemporary literature and morality expressed in *Satire* 1 is followed by further intolerant condemnation of these and other faults in his remaining satires. Throughout, the ideals of independence and self-reliance are asserted in uncompromising terms, drawn from an extreme, hard-line version of the Stoic philosophy, which is Persius' chosen idiom.

Persius' sixth *Satire* is presented as an epistle (following the tradition of Lucilius and Horace: see Chapter 7) in which withdrawal from Rome to the coast is the logical consequence and physical realisation of the isolation proclaimed throughout his book of satires, a violent, symbolic expression of independence and detachment from society and its obligations. The harsh, aggressive attitude adopted throughout the book is turned upon his heir in this poem right to the end of the book:

> But YOU, my heir,
> whoever you are, come a bit further from the crowd and listen.

(6.41-2)

> Do you say no? You'd better take what's left and be grateful.
> 'There's something missing from the total.' I spent a bit on
>   myself,
> but whatever is there is all yours. Don't bother asking the
>   whereabouts
> of the sum Tadius left to me long ago, and don't keep saying,
>   'Write down your inheritance
> from your father, add the revenue of interest, subtract the expenses,

what's left?' Left? Come on, boy, pour the oil on my greens,
pour it on more lavishly. On holidays do you suppose that
    I'll have
boiled nettles and smoked pig's cheek split through the ear,
so that that wild descendant of yours, stuffed with goose
    innards,
can some day piss into a patrician cunt when his pernickety vein
sobs in his roving groin? Or that I'll be left with a thread-bare
figure, while HIS priest-belly wobbles with fat?

                                     (6. 63-74)

An end to anger?

Herein lies the chief difference between Persius and Juvenal. Persius'
speaker remains an isolationist to the end, deeply entrenched in his
isolation which is represented graphically in *Satire* 6 by his withdrawal
from Rome and his couldn't-care-less attitude. By contrast, in Juvenal
the angry speaker situates himself within society. Not only does he
remain in the city, he presents himself standing on the street corner,
fulminating against the outrages that surround him. E.g.:

                       For who could be so inured
to the wicked city, so dead to feeling, as to keep his temper
when the brand-new litter of Matho the lawyer heaves in sight,
filled with himself...

                                     (1.30-3)

and:

There, at the intersection, wouldn't you like to fill
a large-size notebook when a figure comes by on six pairs of
    shoulders
in a litter exposed on this side and that and almost indecent,
recalling in many ways the limp and sprawling Maecenas,
a forger of wills who has turned himself into a wealthy
    gentleman
with the simple aid of a sheet of paper and a moistened signet?
Here is a high-born lady, who just before handing her husband
some mellow Calenian adds a dash of shrivelling toad.

                                     (1.63-70)

And, from the climax to *Satire* 6:

> Every morning you meet Eriphyles in dozens, and also
> daughters of Danaus; every street has a Clytemnestra.
>
> (6.655-6)

The exception is Umbricius in *Satire* 3, who takes his anger to its logical conclusion and withdraws from society by physically withdrawing from the city of Rome. That's why his condemnation of the wicked city is delivered to his friend (who will stay behind in the city of sin!) in the grove of Egeria at the city gate, a grove which itself is already corrupted by an invasion of Jewish beggars, symbolising the problems of the city as a whole (3.12-20). And that's why *Satire* 3 closes with his departure along the Appian Way (3.315-22), ironically heading towards a Greek destination on the Bay of Naples which is more Roman than the un-Roman city.

Persius brings his angry satire to an end by removing his angry satirist from Rome. (That is, if *Satire* 6 was intended as the closing poem to the book. According to one ancient tradition, Persius died before completing his book of satires.) Juvenal leaves his angry satirist in the city to the end, but marks his departure from angry satire in a different way. In the course of *Satires* 1-6, that is, Books 1 and 2, he has confronted his angry citizen with a wide range of 'outrages' guaranteed to make his blood boil. The focus in *Satires* 1-5 (Book 1) is upon public life and, it therefore follows, primarily upon men, men functioning in society as clients and patrons, as wielders of power and as victims of power. *Satire* 6, the single poem which makes up Book 2, complements this with its focus upon private life and particularly upon Roman wives. In Book 1 the angry man reveals his homophobia (hatred of homosexuals) and racism and other bigotries. In Book 2 he adds misogyny to this list. And he does this in an astonishing rant of epic dimensions: the poem is nearly 700 lines long, the same length as a book of the *Aeneid*, a length unparalleled within Roman satire. By the end of *Satire* 6, then, Juvenal has presented a really wide-ranging portrayal of the angry citizen. He has exhausted the artistic possibilities of anger. So he needs to bring this venture in angry satire to a close. He does so not by banishing his satirist (as Persius had done) but by depicting him as going far too far. This happens in the closing lines, starting with the speaker's claim that satire replaces tragedy (6.634-7, quoted above in Chapter 1). He goes on to make the extravagant claim that his modern-day tragedy of the wickedness of Roman wives is worse than any literary one (6.638-46, 651-661) – a really extravagant claim. And this extravagance is emphasised by his criticism of women at this point for their uncontrolled anger with an inflated epic-style simile:

> Extreme atrocities tend
> to cause less shock when fury incites the female to outrage,
> and when, with their hearts inflamed by madness, they are
>   carried down
> like boulders wrenched from a mountain ridge as the ground
>   collapses
> and the vertical face falls in from beneath the hanging cliff-top.
>
> (6.646-50)

The injustice of this is obvious: if there is anyone here who is exhibiting uncontrolled anger, it is him. Juvenal has made his angry speaker irredeemable and, with that, concludes his venture in indignation.

Chapter 3
The Mocking Satirist

Laughter and mockery in satire

It has been realised for a long time that the later satires of Juvenal are not delivered by an angry voice. This was the reason why the nineteenth century scholar Otto Ribbeck labelled the later poems as spurious. It is now agreed that such a drastic step is unnecessary and that Juvenal is using a different *persona* for his later works. This *persona* is that of a laughing satirist with a superior tone of voice: he is mocking the world from a detached vantage-point of superiority and immunity. Unlike the angry mask, which is situated right in the centre of society, responding to it passionately, the laughing, mocking satirist surveys the world from on high. It is easiest to appreciate this by looking at a well-known poem of Juvenal which shows this approach, *Satire* 10. This mask is not Juvenal's invention. Its foundations were there in Horace and, after establishing the mocking mask of Juvenal's *Satire* 10, this chapter will proceed to consider Horace's handling of mockery.

Democritus and Juvenal Satire 10

The key to understanding difference between passionate involvement in the world and dispassionate mockery is clearly and succinctly presented in the programmatic opening section of *Satire* 10, the poem which inspired Samuel Johnson's *The Vanity of Human Wishes* (published in 1749). After introducing as the theme of the poem the lack of basis for people's fears and desires (5), Juvenal indicates two possible approaches by drawing analogies with two early Greek philosophers, Democritus and Heraclitus:

> In view of that, you may well approve of the two philosophers:
> one of them used to laugh whenever he closed the door
> and stepped into the street; his opposite number would weep.
> (10.28-30)

As he proceeds, we see which of these approaches he is sympathetic with:

> While harsh censorious laughter is universal and easy,
> one wonders how the other's eyes were supplied with moisture.
> Democritus' sides would shake with gales of incessant laughter,
> although in the towns of his day there were no purple- or scarlet-
> bordered togas to be seen; no rods or litters or platforms.
>
> (31-5)

He then depicts a Roman ceremonial occasion which he suggests would have made Democritus laugh even more. Democritus' irreverent attitude to similar material afforded by his own society and times is then described:

> In his day too, in all the places where people gathered,
> he found material for laughter. He showed by his excellent sense
> that men of the highest quality who will set the finest examples
> may be born in a land with a thick climate, peopled by boneheads.
> He used to laugh at the masses' worries, and at their pleasures,
> and sometimes, too, at their tears. For himself, when Fortune
>   threatened,
> he would tell her go hang, and make a sign with his middle
>   finger.
>
> (47-53)

So we have a programmatic declaration of the detached and aloof mode of satire: Juvenal adopts the mask of the mocking satirist. And this is borne out by the rest of the poem. It amounts to a clear rejection of the angry mask adopted in the early satires (see Chapter 2). Not only are the marks of indignation, present throughout *Satires* 1-6 (discussed above), absent from *Satire* 10, but the poem has a very clear structure, to suggest it is the product of a rational mind which is fully in control. The various topics of power (56-113), eloquence (114-32), military success (133-87), long life (188-288) and beauty (289-345) are introduced by what amount to headings, and in each section the failing is exposed in a tone of superior mockery. At the end of the poem the satirist mocks the entire process of prayer (346-53) and although he appears to offer positive advice here, it is couched in a context which renders it ridiculous:

> Still, that you may have something to ask for – some reason to offer
> the holy sausages and innards of a little white pig in a chapel –
> you ought to pray for a healthy mind in a healthy body.
>
> (354-6)

The rejection of anger which follows signifies Juvenal's change from his earlier indignant *persona*:

> Ask for a valiant heart which has banished fear of death,
> which looks upon length of days as one of the least of nature's
> gifts; which is able to suffer every kind of hardship,
> is proof against anger, craves for nothing, and reckons the trials
> and gruelling labours of Hercules as more desirable blessings
> than the amorous ease and the banquets and cushions of
> Sardanapallus.
>
> (357-62)

And in the final words, the satirist takes over Democritus' mocking attitude to Fortune by declaring her to be a human projection and not a goddess in her own right.

Juvenal's use of Democritus as an archetype of the mask of mocking superiority is inspired by a passage in Horace's *Epistle to Augustus* in which Horace pillories the enthusiasm for stage-shows:

> If he were still on earth, Democritus would laugh,
> whether it were a giraffe (that cross-breed of camel and leopard)
> or a white elephant that attracted the gaze of the crowd.
> He'd watch the crowd more closely than the show itself –
> it offered him more sights worth seeing by far.
> But the writers he'd think were telling their stories
> to a deaf ass. For what voice was ever strong enough
> to overcome the din that arises in our theatres?
>
> (*Ep.* 2.1.194-201)

Juvenal takes this seed and develops it. But when we look at Horace's own work, we can see that this mask features in his satirical writings from the start.

Them and Us in Horace

The elements of superiority are visible in a poem which mostly uses the self-ironic approach (which will be discussed in next chapter), Horace *Satires* 1.5, often known as the 'Journey to Brindisi'. The poem is about 'them and us'. The 'us' is the élite group around Maecenas, the group which Horace wishes to impress so that he will be included in it. The poem therefore celebrates the standards of the group. Part of this celebration consists of mockery of those who fail to reach such standards. It is significant, then, that the first instance of overt mockery occurs immediately after Maecenas has joined the group, when a 'crazy official' is pilloried (31-6). The centre-piece of the poem is the contest between two rustic buffoons (51-70). Through his criticism of the crude, out-and-out insults bandied by the two buffoons in the name of entertainment, Horace is indirectly suggesting that his mode of critique is superior: *he* would not indulge in anything so vulgar! (And perhaps there is also an implicit contrast between the slanging match and satire itself, with the suggestion that satire is more subtle than crude name-calling. Self-referentiality like this occurs elsewhere in the Satires.) This incident is immediately followed by yet another which reveals the sense of superiority of the travelling party:

> From there we made straight for Beneventum, where our fussy
>   host
> almost went up in flames while turning some lean thrushes on
>   the fire:
> Vulcan slipped out and his flickering flame immediately
> shot through the ancient kitchen to lick the roof-top.
> Then you would have seen the hungry guests and frightened
>   slaves
> grabbing the dinner and everyone struggling to put out the blaze.
>
> (71-6)

The absence of sympathy for the predicament of the 'fussy host' is a clear mark of the superior mask adopted by Horace here.

This incident is a foretaste of a more extended example of the same phenomenon in *Satires* 2.8, aptly called 'the feast of fools' by Freudenburg (*The Walking Muse* p. 234). This poem is a dialogue between Horace and the comic poet Fundanius. Horace asks Fundanius to recount to him the dinner-party which he (Fundanius) attended with Maecenas the previous day. Fundanius is happy to oblige and delivers a narrative which mocks the efforts of the host, Nasidienus Rufus, to impress his important guests. What Fundanius finds particularly offensive is the way Nasidienus parades his learning about food. For example:

> First there was Lucanian boar. It was caught in a gentle southerly
> breeze, as the father of the feast kept telling us.
>
> (6-7)

Mocking phrases like 'the father of the feast' here and 'his lordship' at 16 and 43 convey Fundanius' sense of superiority. The unwanted information about food is provided by Nomentanus, Nasidienus' client, who was deputed to tell the 'uninitiated mob' about the special quality of the food served (25-33), and throughout by the host himself, for example:

> his lordship remarked ,'This [lamprey] was caught
> while pregnant; its flesh is inferior after spawning.
> The ingredients of the sauce are these: Venafran oil (from the first
> pressing), fish-sauce (from the juices of Spanish mackerel),
> wine five years old, but produced in Italy,
> to be added while it is on the boil (after boiling, Chian suits
> better than anything else); white pepper, and not forgetting
> vinegar made from fermenting the Methymnean grape.
> I was the first to demonstrate incorporating sharp bitter elecampane
> and green rockets into the boiling sauce; Curtillus would use
>   sea-urchins
> unwashed, because the liquid from the shell-fish is better than
>   brine.'
>
> (43-53)

At this point disaster strikes Nasidienus, in the shape of a collapsing awning. Fundanius' inappropriate epic-style description of the incident marks his mocking detachment from the scene (54-6). The host's reaction is an over-reaction: he weeps 'as if his son had died young' (58-9). His client Nomentanus consoles him as if for a real loss in grandiose language (61-3) which is picked up by one of Maecenas' entourage who delivers an elaborate mock-consolation, full of superior irony (65-74), for example:

> But as with a general so with a host: adverse circumstances
> usually reveal his genius whereas good luck obscures it.
>
> (73-4)

The mockery is lost on Nasidienus, who accepts the consolation as if it were genuine (75-6). Horace here interrupts Fundanius' narrative, pointing up the content and drawing attention to the mockery:

> There's no other show I'd rather have seen.
> But go on, what was the next laugh?
>
> (79-80)

The final scene at this wretched dinner-party occurs when Nasidienus re-enters, 'resolved on mending disaster by cleverness' (85). Fundanius himself admits that the food produced at this point – blackbirds and pigeons – would have been perfectly acceptable, had Nasidienus not 'given a lecture on their origins and properties' (92-3). The group of superior diners finally take their revenge on the host for continually and inappropriately ramming knowledge down their throats:

> ... by running away
> without tasting a thing, as if the food had been blighted
> by Canidia's breath, more deadly than African snakes.
>
> (93-5)

Throughout *Satires* 2.8, Nasidienus is the butt of humour, both at the dinner-party itself and in Fundanius' account of it. Clearly Nasidienus can be seen as a social climber, a *nouveau riche*, who is so intent on impressing his important guests that he takes it too far, especially in his insistence on the unusualness of the food served and on his expertise in choice (in which he resembles the pretentious Catius of *Satires* 2.4, discussed in Chapter 4). But at the same time, another perspective is possible too. Nasidienus' guests exhibit bad manners throughout the meal. For example, some of them try to 'drink him out of the house' (33-41) and (as we have seen) one of them mocks him with an ironical consolation for the disaster of the fallen awning. The climax of bad manners is the abrupt and premature departure of the entire group without waiting to taste the food. The conduct of these guests throughout marks them as behaving in a condescending way.

This condescending and snobbish attitude is underlined by the way Fundanius – who clearly endorses and identifies with the sensibilities of the group – narrates the incident to Horace. It is no accident that Fundanius is a *comic* poet – exactly the kind of person from whom we might expect to hear a funny story. His first words hint at this (3-4): 'I've never had a better time in all my life.' It is not only the occasion itself but the opportunity to describe it which he relishes. Horace later underlines this by describing Fundanius' narrative as better than any show (78). Horace's choice of narrator is clever, but he is not absolved by this choice. He is complicit, in his initial invitation to Fundanius to furnish the humorous details (1-3) and in his further encouragements to extract all the details (18-19, where he ironically describes the dinner-party as a 'magnificent occasion'; and 79-80, quoted above). Fundanius and Horace share the same condescending, mocking laughter at the expense of the pretentious host Nasidienus.

Satirical superiority

These are not the only poems of Horace in which he uses the mask of the mocking satirist, but they are typical. The central characteristic of the mocking satirist is his sense of superiority over his victims. This may consist of intellectual or moral superiority, as in the case of Juvenal's Democritean satirist in *Satire* 10, or it may consist of social superiority, as in the cases examined in Horace's *Satires*. This superiority goes along with a pose of detachment, in contrast with the angry satirist who is typically situated in a seething city setting surrounded by outrageous people. The satirists who laugh and mock do so from the quiet of their studies, from their rich houses or country retreats. A further contrast between these two types of satirist is in the objects of their criticisms. Whereas the angry satirist is likely to be enraged by acts of wickedness and criminality, the mocking satirist tends to deride the foolishness of humankind. And, finally, there is a contrast in the ways the two kinds of satire work on the audience – on us. The angry mask of satire attempts to arouse our emotions by its own emotional appeal and to sweep us into agreement. By contrast, the mocking mask of satire tries to seduce us into wanting to join an exclusive club. But it is worth looking carefully at the basis of this élitism: what standards are we claiming for ourselves if we endorse the views of the foolishness of humankind which are expressed by the mocking satirist? Do we want to be associated with such a snob? The mocking mask of satire has no chink of humility or humanity; it is cruel in its condemnation.

Chapter 4
The Smiling Satirist

Horace's ironic smile

Only one of the Roman satirists merits the title of the smiling satirist. Persius' characterisation of 'Horace' is highly accurate:

> The rascal Flaccus touches every fault in his friend while
> he laughs and, once he's got in, he frolics around his heart,
> clever at hanging the public from his cleared nose.
>
> (Persius, *Satire* 1.116-18)

Humour and humility are the keys to Horace's approach. He presents an unthreatening appearance through self-deprecation and invitations to laughter at his own expense, but at the same time offers criticisms, often indirect, which take his victims and his audience unawares. His stance of humility emerges strongly from *Satires* 1.4 and 1.6. In 1.4 he excludes himself from the number of poets (1.4.39-44), and in arguing that he is not malevolent (1.4.78-102) derives his code of morality from his father, in particular his father's practice of pointing out good and bad examples to be followed and avoided (1.4.105-26). In Roman terms, this approach is commendable: a son's deference to his father is a reinforcement of the role of the *paterfamilias* as head of the household. And in literary terms, this amounts to a clever satiric strategy. Horace refuses the role of aggressor and instead portrays himself as on the defensive against unjustified allegations, but then delivers indirect criticisms, which he (implicitly) endorses by attributing them to his father.

He uses a similar strategy of humility in *Satires* 1.6, where he emphasises his own lowly origins (a classic satiric strategy, explained by Freudenburg *The Walking Muse* p. 213) and praises the social mobility practised by Maecenas who (he claims) judges people on their intrinsic qualities, not on their external, inherited trappings:

> Now to return to myself – only a freedman's son,
> criticised by everyone as only a freedman's son,
> *now*, because I'm an associate of yours, Maecenas, *before*,

because as a military tribune I had a Roman legion under my
command.
The two cases are different: though someone might reasonably
grudge me that rank, he shouldn't grudge me your friendship
as well,
especially as you are careful to choose only suitable people
and to keep away from unscrupulous self-seeking.

(1.6.45-52)

This humility enables him to criticise the lives, aspirations and prejudices
of ambitious people through endorsing Maecenas' view of the world.
This continues the strategy of *Satires* 1.4, with Maecenas here in the role
of the father-figure who is rendered responsible for the moral judgements
delivered in the poem.

Humility and humour

Horace's humility is blended with humour. A prime example is the joke
at the end of *Satires* 1.4. One of the recurring themes of the poem is what
it is to be a poet. Early in the poem, he excludes himself 'from those who
can properly be called poets' (39-42), suggesting that there is an important distinction between lowly, prosaic comedy and satire on the one
hand and elevated epic on the other (43-62). But towards the end he
admits as one of his 'milder faults' that he likes to amuse himself on
paper (138-40). The joke comes at the end when he threatens to set the
(enormous) company of poets onto anyone who wants to interfere with
his poetic activities (140-3). This self-ironic inconsistency provides a
light-hearted touch at the end which in turn reinforces his image as a
smiling satirist. And this is far from unique: very frequently we find Horace
closing a satire with a slightly destabilising and disconcerting 'joke'. For
example, *Satires* 1.9 ends with a literary joke (discussed below), *Satires*
2.1 with a pun on the different senses of *carmina* ('songs' or 'spells'),
Epistles 1.4 with a self-ironic reference to himself as 'a hog from
Epicurus' herd' (discussed below), and the so-called *Ars Poetica* with a
startling and humorous image of the poet as a madman, behaving like a
bear that has smashed the bars of its cage or like a leech sucking the blood
of his audience and reading them to death.

This playfulness operates on a larger scale too, at times. A good
example of how Horace uses irony at his own expense to amuse us and
put us off our guard is *Satires* 1.9, often known as 'The Pest'. Horace
narrates an incident which he claims happened to him as he was strolling

through Rome. As the 'pest' begins his dogged pursuit of Horace, intent on using him as a means of introduction into the circle of Horace's powerful patron Maecenas, we learn how difficult Horace found it to shake him off:

> Desperately trying to get away
> I now quickened my pace, sometimes stopped,
> then whispered a word in my slave's ear, while the sweat was
>   trickling
> right down to my ankles. As he babbled on, praising the streets
> and the whole city, I kept muttering to myself
> 'Bolanus, how I envy you your temper!'
>
> (8-13)

His portrayal of his inability to express his annoyance is the first of many details critical of himself. Another is where he compares himself to a donkey, hardly a flattering comparison, by Roman standards or our own:

> My ears drooped like a sulky donkey when he's had too heavy
> a load put on his back.
>
> (20-1)

Again, the mock-epic tone of the fortune-teller's prediction of Horace's future fate underlines the humour at his own expense:

> 'Him no deadly poison or foeman's steel shall carry off
> nor painful pleurisy or cough or slow-foot gout;
> a chatterbox shall wear him out, whenever his time comes:
> if he is wise, as he grows older, he'll avoid the talkative.'
>
> (31-4)

The gulf between the elevated tone and the mundane content, together with the exaggeration in the idea that to meet a 'chatterbox' could be fatal, combine to invite mockery of Horace. This lavish use of ironic self-criticism makes it unsurprising that Horace deploys irony against the pest a little later:

> 'You're inflaming my desire to get really close
> to him.' You only have to make the wish. With your excellent
>   qualities
> you'll take him by storm. He's a man who can be conquered –
> and that's why

he makes the initial approaches difficult. 'I won't let myself
down.

> I'll bribe his slaves; and if I'm shut out
> today, I'll persevere; I'll wait for the right moment,
> I'll waylay him in the street, I'll escort him home. "To mortals
> life gives nothing without great toil." '

(53-60)

This creates a further dimension of humour, since the pest is (of course)
too insensitive to react to the irony of 'your excellent qualities' and so
on, but interprets Horace's words at face-value (or, at least, ignores their
ironic potential). In fact, Horace's indirect, ironic approach is utterly
useless against an opponent as brash and blatant as this pest. So his irony
at his own expense continues. At this point, his friend Aristius Fuscus
comes up and despite Horace's efforts deliberately refuses to understand
his predicament or help him out of it:

> I began tugging at his sleeve,
> squeezing his arm (which remained impassive), nodding,
> swivelling my eyes to say, 'Get me *out* of here!' The cruel joker
> smiled and pretended not to understand. My temper blazed.
> 'You definitely said there was something or other you wanted
> to discuss
> with me in private.' 'I remember it well, but I'll tell you
> at a better time.'

(63-9)

The ultimate irony is that Horace is finally preserved from the pest only
by the mock-epic intervention of Apollo (based on a scene in Homer's
Iliad, 20.443) to take away the pest to the law-case he has been neglecting
in favour of cultivating Horace as an entrée to Maecenas' circle.

The indirectness of irony

Horace's ironic approach – which involves laughing at himself and
inviting others to join in that laughter – makes for indirect satire. But at
the same time this is effective satire at the pest's expense too. The pest
is satirised for being a social climber, for being totally unscrupulous
about how he can get into Maecenas' circle, for totally misunderstanding
(according to Horace at any rate) the criteria for being valued there. This
poem, then, delivers satire on anyone who shares the social ambitions
and attitudes of the pest. This is a seductive type of satire because we are

readily persuaded into adopting Horace's viewpoint: the narrative is controlled by Horace and we never hear the pest's own version of the narrative. It's also seductive because it's more appealing to hear criticism from someone with apparent humility than from someone who bursts in raging brashly (see Chapter 2).

The same kind of strategy is worked out in *Satires* 2.4, but this time with the equivalent of the 'pest' present, in conversation with Horace. The 'pest' here is Catius, stopped in the street by Horace as he rushes away from a lecture on gastronomy to write down the words of wisdom he's just heard. The opening dialogue has an irony, the force of which only becomes fully appreciated later:

> Catius! Where have you been and where are you off to? 'No
>   time to stop. I must
> make notes of these new teachings which are going to outdo
> Pythagoras and the man Anytus accused and the learned Plato.'
> I know it's wrong of me to stop you at such an awkward
> moment, but be good enough to forgive me, please.
> But if anything just now slips your mind you'll soon recall it;
> whether it's a natural gift or a skill, you're a marvel.
> 'Well that was exactly my concern, how I might keep it all in
>   my mind,
> because it was a subtle theme handled in a subtle style.'
> Tell me the man's name. Is he a Roman or a visitor?
> 'The teachings I'll recite from memory; the professor's name
>   must remain a secret.
> When serving eggs remember...'
>
>   (1-12)

And so Catius repeats the whole lengthy lecture to Horace – and the lecture turns out to be a parody of philosophical lectures on the good life. This leads Horace to say at the end:

> What a clever man you are, Catius! In the name of our
>   friendship and the gods,
> do remember to take me to hear the next lecture, wherever it is
>   you go.
> For however retentive your memory when you relate it all to me,
> yet as an interpreter you cannot delight me as much. *And*
> there's the man's expression and appearance. *You* don't think
>   it important

> to see him because you are lucky enough to have had that
>   privilege, but I
> have no ordinary desire to be able to approach those far-off
>   fountains
> and to drink from there the teachings of the happy life.
>   (88-95)

The irony of the phrase 'clever man' here is clear and informs Horace's praise of Catius' memory earlier. And the irony of the reference to 'the happy life' picks up Catius' straightforward praise of the lecture as 'new teachings which are going to outdo Pythagoras and the man Anytus accused [Socrates] and the learned Plato' (2-3). Horace smiles at Catius, but the irony here is at Catius' expense. The smiling allows satiric indirectness which is actually fiercely critical of the unwitting victim but which requires understanding and complicity from the audience, who must share the ironist's perspective for the irony to work successfully.

The dramatic situation of this and several other poems in *Satires* 2 bears a strong resemblance to that of the pest poem (*Satires* 1.9). In all these poems, Horace has to listen to the thoughts and obsessions of someone who shows himself to be a fool. In *Satires* 2.4, there is perhaps less emphasis upon the irony at Horace's expense; but both 2.3 and 2.7 close with personal attacks upon Horace for his faults, and his angry reaction indicates that he invites us to see these attacks as justified! For example, in 2.7 his slave Davus inflicts on Horace a third-hand Stoic lecture on the nature of freedom and then dares to criticise his master:

>   'What's more,
>   you can't endure even an hour of your own company,
>   you don't invest your free time properly and you avoid yourself
>   like a runaway
>   or truant slave, attempting to elude Angst with wine or sleep:
>   without success, since that black companion dogs and chases
>   you as you run away.'
>   'Where can I get a stone?' 'What for?' 'Where are my arrows?'
>   'The man's either delirious – or versifying!' 'If you don't get
>   out of here
>   right away, you'll be labourer number nine on my Sabine farm!'
>   (2.7.111-8)

Again, this demonstrates the subtlety of the smiling, ironic satirist. He can portray himself as on the receiving end of some of life's little trials while at the same time allowing the people around him to demonstrate their follies and faults. In this way, the satirist remains in control without that control being obvious.

The last example of the smiling satirist in Horace is *Epistles* 1.4. This brief poem takes the form of a letter addressed to Albius, probably the love elegist Albius Tibullus (writing in the 20s BC, died 19 BC). Tibullus has evidently been suffering from depression – something which has to be inferred from the text, given the usual subtlety of the epistle form which provides only one side of a conversation but enables us to reconstruct the other element of the 'dialogue' between Horace and his addressees (for full discussion of the different forms of Roman satire see Chapter 7).

> Albius, impartial judge of my 'conversations',
> what shall I say you are doing in your country haunts at Pedum?
> Writing something to outdo the efforts of Cassius of Parma
> or strolling quietly through the healthy woods,
> pondering on everything that suits someone wise and good?
> You never were a body without a soul. The gods
> have given you good looks, wealth and the capacity of enjoyment.
> What more could a nurse wish for her darling baby
> if he could show good sense and express his feelings and had
> in abundance influence, reputation and health
> and a decent standard of living with a never-failing wallet?
> Among hopes and anxieties, fear and anger,
> think that every day that dawns is your last;
> the hour you never hoped for will arrive as a welcome surprise.
> As for me, when you want a laugh, come and see me: I'm fat
>   and sleek,
> in peak condition, a hog from Epicurus' herd.
>
> (*Epistles* 1.4)

The letter offers affectionate advice in a smiling and friendly tone. This makes possible the giving of advice, namely, that Tibullus should recognise his advantages and live life to the full each day. Any danger of this seeming pompous or impertinent is removed by the final suggestion in the last two lines (15-16). Here Horace's self-irony persists; the humour at his own expense has a certain self-reflexive function. By describing himself as 'a hog from Epicurus' herd' Horace acknowledges that the advice he has just given is Epicurean in flavour without necessarily implying that he is a follower or advocate of Epicureanism. This is confirmed by a broader view of the twenty poems of *Epistles* 1 in which he clearly shifts his philosophical angle according to the needs of the moment, usually in response to the addressee's situation and mood. Moreover, at the start of Epistles 1.1 he explicitly claims to be eclectic (lines 13-19).

The seduction of playfulness

The advantages of adopting a smiling and ironic mask in satire are by now clear. Horace's playfulness – especially at his own expense – makes him seem very unthreatening. This provides a secure basis from which to deliver criticism. Moreover, the criticism seems indirect and takes the audience – and its victims – unawares. Yet at the same time this playfulness indirectly asserts Horace's power. He is in charge. He can construct a coherent case and then raise doubts about it. Just when we think we know what a particular poem has been 'about', Horace destabilises it and with it our assumptions, by closing with a joke or piece of self-irony which leaves us to question the seriousness of what preceded it. Unlike the angry satirist, who can easily alienate us because of his lack of self-control, and unlike the mocking satirist, who can easily alienate us because of his superiority, the smiling satirist seems seductively unthreatening and because of that the power of his criticism is increased. Persius could hardly have been more accurate in his assessment of how Horatian satire operates.

Chapter 5
The Good, The Bad and The Ugly

The satirist as witch-doctor and as murderer

To see satire as drama (as argued in Chapter 1) immediately sets it in an explicitly social context. The satirist takes on the role of the defender of society's norms by criticising deviations from those norms in what he claims to be a manner sanctioned by society. This kind of role is familiar from many cultures. In his important book *The Power of Satire* (1960) Robert Elliott suggests that the satirist is a descendant of the witch-doctors of primitive societies, whose power lay in the spells and curses which they could use to drive out deviant elements. This approach invites an alignment between Roman satire and native Italian traditions of abuse which seem to have fulfilled a regulatory function by attacking extreme behaviour, such as the apotropaic* songs ('turning away' the evil spirits associated with pride) at the expense of triumphing generals (to avert the 'evil eye') and the *flagitatio*, which was the public shaming of a wrong-doer, and perhaps the so-called fescennine verses (another kind of apotropaic song) associated with wedding ritual and other rites of passage. All were socially approved modes of criticism. Roman culture, then, appears to have had a long and strong tradition of public ways of moderating extreme behaviour and it looks as if the role of society's moral spokesman adopted in Roman satire readily fits into that slot – at least that's what satirists like to claim, because it justifies their expressions of hostility to claim to be socially useful.

But at the same time, satirists are well aware that they are criticised for being anti-social in their aggression. Two stories about early Greek iambic* poets express graphically society's fears about the satirist's power with words. Archilochus of Paros (7th century BC) belonged to a family of priests of Demeter but his mother was a slave. He became engaged to the daughter of the noble Lycambes. But when Lycambes discovered Archilochus was the son of a slave he withdrew his daughter from the marriage contract. In a rage, Archilochus composed iambic poems against Lycambes and his household and recited them at the festival of Demeter. The result was tragic: Lycambes and and his daughter hanged themselves. A similar story is told of Hipponax of

Ephesus (6th century BC). He was a small, misshapen man who was sensitive about his appearance. Two sculptors made a statue of him, exaggerating his deformity and ridiculing him. Hipponax retaliated in iambic poetry and (according to some accounts) the two sculptors committed suicide.

In this chapter I shall examine some of the images used to explore and express the satirist's role in society. Hero, saint, judge, preacher, doctor, surgeon, cleanser and detective – these are some of the positive images. Negative images include the villain, the hooligan, the criminal and the sadist. Most of these images centre upon the satirist's (real or perceived) aggression and that therefore will be my focus here. The crucial quotations from Roman satire are all drawn from passages where the satirist defends himself from attack.

Favourable imagery

The most positive representation of the satirist's aggression is to heroise it. The satirist as hero is easy to find. Lucilius, the founder of the genre of Roman satire, is portrayed by Juvenal as an epic hero steering his chariot across the plain:

> But why, you may ask, should I decide to cover the ground
> o'er which the mighty son of Aurunca drove his team?
>
> *(Sat.* 1.19-20)

The image is presented more explicitly at the end of the same poem:

> Whenever, as though with sword in hand, the hot Lucilius
> roars in wrath, the listener flushes; his mind is affrighted
> with a sense of sin, and his conscience sweats with secret guilt.
>
> (1.165-7)

In Juvenal's imagery, the satirist is a warrior, wielding his sword on behalf of society. But this imagery is not original to Juvenal. Earlier, Horace offered this self-defence against the allegation of aggression:

> But this point and pen will not attack
> any living being, unless provoked, and it will protect me, like
> a sword
> hidden in its scabbard. Why should I try to draw it
> so long as I'm safe from marauding thugs? O Jupiter,
> father and king, may my unused weapon be destroyed by rust

and may no one injure a peace-loving man like me. But whoever
rouses me (better not touch, I'm telling you!) will be sorry
and will be talked about through the whole city, notorious.

(*Satires* 2.1.39-46)

The role of the epic hero implies a moral superiority which serves as a
justification for the satirist's aggression, as well as justifying the appropriation by satire of the epic hexameter metre (discussed in Chapter 6).
This image links with other positive images of the satirist which likewise
involve the removal of bad features of human behaviour. When the
satirist takes on the role of cleanser or doctor or surgeon, the vices of
society are the dirt or the disease or the rot that needs to be removed or
cured or cut out. So Horace praises Lucilius 'for scouring Rome with his
abundant salty wit' (*Sat.* 1.10.4) and Persius is described as 'scraping
delicate ears with the biting truth' (1.107-8).

Unfavourable imagery

Those are some of the favourable images; there are unfavourable images,
too, chiefly involving an allegation of aggression. For example, the
satirist is typically accused of slander and libel. His lawyer friend
Trebatius gives Horace a warning of these dangers:

If a party compose
harmful verses against anyone, there is the law
and a trial.

(*Sat.* 2.1.81-3)

This conversation may be inspired by an earlier poem of Lucilius, of
which two fragments survive, in which Lucilius appears to be attacked :

You enjoy it when you spread around those bad reports about
me in your conversations.

and you split me apart by libelling me in many of your
conversations.

(1085 and 1086W)

Worse than the accusation of malicious verbal aggression is the accusation of physical violence. Persius says:

Lucilius ripped into Rome –

you, Lupus, you, Mucius, and smashed his back tooth on them.

(1.114-15)

This image is perhaps supported by fragments of Lucilius such as this one:

Then let me launch myself at him with a dog's gape and gaze.

(1000-1W)

Dogs bark. Dogs bite. Dogs also shit. So satirists are accused of defiling the world. Persius, for example, is advised not to defecate or urinate on 'sacred' ground:

'Here,' you say, 'I forbid the voiding of excrement.'
Draw two snakes: 'Lads, this place is off limits; piss outside.'

(1.112-14)

On this view, satire is a form of bodily discharge and the satirist is like a dog or a hooligan, defacing society.

The satirist as chimney-sweep

It is obvious that these two types of image of the satirist's aggression, favourable and unfavourable, conflict. Is it possible to reconcile these images? Is the satirist a hero or a hooligan – the good guy or the bad guy? The answer is both and neither. The ambivalence of the satirist's position emerges from numerous passages in Roman satire but is most succinctly captured in two stanzas of the *Whipper Pamphlets* (an anonymous attack on a satirist dating from 1601):

Behold, thou misconceyuing *Satyrist*,
The quaffing ale-knight hath a reeling pace:
The Cobler alwaies shewes a durtie fist:
Who liues a Smith, must needs besmere his face.
Then know, thou filthy sweepe-chimney of sin,
The soyle thereof defiles thy soule within.

O wonder great! Is it not villany,
That one should liue by reckning vp of vice,
And be a sinne-monger professedly,
Inuoluming offences for a price?

Yet by the same doth purchase but the shame,
And blaming others, merits others blame.
                              (*The Whipping of the Satyre* 175-86)

The satirist is the chimney-sweep of sin: he cleans, but gets dirty in the process and so by 'blaming others, merits others blame'. The question, ultimately, is who the others are. He is the good guy if we agree with his 'blaming' and the bad guy if we don't – in which case we are likely to 'blame' him. Our view of the satirist is crucially bound up with our personal reaction to what the satirist says (or seems to say). So, perhaps, in the end, the satirist is simply ugly. The process of exposing some of the silly and horrible aspects of human behaviour without acknow-ledging any redeeming features inevitably sets the satirist apart, even when he depicts himself as in the middle of society.

Chapter 6
The Satirist as Authority Figure

The graphic realism of satire

Consider these two pictures of life in Rome, one written under Augustus and the other some 130 years later, under Trajan or Hadrian:

> Apart from all that, do you reckon I can write poetry
> in Rome when I have so many worries and so many tasks?
> One man wants me to be his sponsor, another to abandon
> all my duties and listen to his writings; this one is ill in bed
> on the Quirinal, that one on the far side of the Aventine; both must be
> visited. The distances you see are helpfully convenient! 'Yes, but
> the streets are clear, so there's no obstacle to composition.'
> A feverish contractor rushes past with his mules and workmen;
> a huge contraption hoists a boulder then a beam;
> mournful funerals struggle their way through the hefty waggons.
> There goes a mad dog; here runs a muddy sow.
> Now, go on and try to compose tuneful verses!
> (Horace *Epistles* 2.2.65-76)

That's the root of the trouble. The coming and going of waggons
in the narrow winding streets, the yells at a halted herd,
would banish sleep from even a seal or the emperor Drusus.
If duty calls, as the crowd falls back, the rich man passes
quickly above their faces in a large Liburnian galley,
reading or writing or taking a nap as he speeds along.
(The closed windows of a litter can make the occupant drowsy.)
Yet he'll arrive before us. As we hurry along we are blocked
by a wave in front; behind, a massive multitude crushes
my pelvis; *he* digs in with an elbow, *he* with a hard-wood
pole; then *he* hits my head with a beam and *he* with a wine-jar.
My legs are caked with mud; from every side I am trampled
by giant feet; a soldier stamps on my toe with his hob-nails.

Look at all that smoke; a crowd is having a picnic.
A hundred guests, each with a portable kitchen behind him.
Corbulo could hardly carry so many enormous utensils,
so many things on his head, as that unfortunate slave-boy,
who keeps his head erect and fans the flame as he runs.

(Juvenal 3.236-53)

Vivid – yes. Plausible – maybe. But real – not necessarily. Readers of
Roman satire have often been taken in by the rhetorical technique known
as *enargeia*, the vivid evocation of a scenario, into thinking that satire
provides an accurate and realistic picture of life in Rome. That's why
satire is used by some textbooks as a rich source of information on
everyday life in Rome. This is a credit to the powers of persuasion of the
authors of Roman satire; but at the same time, it indicates the willingness
of those scholars to believe the lurid pictures of Roman society which
they find in Roman satire! Yet these pictures are characterised by
distortion. The truly 'everyday' features, the mundane and boring features,
are suppressed and omitted or blown out of proportion, and exaggerated
attention is devoted to the extraordinary and the colourful.

I must make it clear that I do not wish to deny that satire can shed
light on the culture that produces it. To deny that would be absurd, and
at the end of this chapter I shall indicate some ways in which Roman
satire can be used to illuminate Roman culture. But we need to find a
way of resisting the satirist's persuasion that his picture is accurate and
realistic. An understanding of how satirical distortion functions is a first
step. This I have provided in the chapter on 'City and country in Roman
Satire' in my *Satire and Society in Ancient Rome*, with special reference
to Juvenal's *Satire* 3. Here I shall develop the point made in Chapter 1
above about the importance of the rhetorical background to Roman
literature. This chapter will show how an appreciation of the education
process shared by members of the Roman élite illuminates the frameworks and some of the details of satiric discourse.

Take a closer look at the two passages quoted above to see how
enargeia works. The cinema is a useful analogy here: satire often has a
cinematic quality which powerfully exercises persuasion and seduction
on its audience. The camera of satire offers city-scape panoramas shot
from vantage-points and chaotic street-scenes shot on the street with the
camera-man being jostled out of the way. One shot follows another so
that they are virtually superimposed (as much as is possible within a piece
of literature where one word has to follow another). Then the camera
zooms in to focus on details, Horace's 'muddy sow' and Juvenal's

'hob-nails' and 'unfortunate slave-boy'. These passages are typical of satire. The jumbled accumulation of vivid details gives an impression of spontaneity which creates an effect of realism and naturalism.

The authority of the satirist

The author of satire, then, produces an effect of realism through careful choice of the objects on which his 'camera' is focussed. But that is not all there is to be said about the camera analogy. Consider too the author's choice of camera-man. Whatever sort of satirist he creates – angry, mocking, or smiling – he invests him with an authority which makes it hard to challenge his picture as unrealistic. This is easiest to see in the case of Juvenal's angry satirist who positions himself with his 'camera' on a Roman street-corner (see Chapter 2 above). Because he is right in the middle of society, with all its silly and horrible people, he claims an immediacy which is designed to validate his picture. The aloof, mocking satirist (such as Juvenal's Democritus: see Chapter 3) is a similarly powerful camera-man. His authority – and hence his implicit truthfulness – derives from the superior status he assumes. His 'camera' is positioned high up with a superhuman, almost divine, perspective. The third type of satirist (examined in Chapter 4) asserts his authority – and with it his claim to accuracy – in a more indirect and subtle way. It is precisely because he is prepared to criticise himself that his criticisms of others are believed. He turns his 'camera' on himself as readily as on others and does not shrink from close-ups. The three masks of satire analysed in Chapters 2, 3 and 4 are all designed to assert authority in their different ways – and a central result of that assertion of authority is a claim, implicit or explicit, that the picture presented is accurate, even that it is the *only* accurate picture. Yet this claim must be resisted: the authority is an index of persuasiveness (in Roman terms, *fides*) and not of accuracy or 'truth'.

Satire and rhetoric

Persuasion was the central aim of the rhetorical education of the Roman élite, as explained in Chapter 1. The claims to realism in Roman satire can be moderated by an appreciation of how the frameworks and features inculcated in the process of rhetorical education shape the poems. 'Rhetoric' tends to be a term of abuse for us – think of the speeches of politicians being rejected as 'just rhetoric' (see Chapter 1). Implicit here is an allegation of lack of sincerity and clever verbal tricks, completely different from the Roman emphasis upon plausibility (*fides*). For the

Romans 'rhetoric' (meaning the whole set of skills which made speech convincing without abandoning the concept of appropriateness, *decorum*) was essential to any man who wanted to play a role in public life. In the field of Roman satire, it is Juvenal who shows most clearly the importance of rhetoric. In E.J. Kenney's words: 'The Satires are pervaded through and through by the influence, not merely of formal rhetorical training, but specifically of the schools of declamation' ('Juvenal: Satirist or Rhetorician?' *Latomus* 22 (1963) 707). A few examples will illustrate this pervasiveness.

On the largest scale the influence of declamation is evident in the choice of subject and framing of ideas (and here I am drawing on important work done by Francis Cairns in *Generic Composition in Greek and Roman Poetry*, Edinburgh, 1972). Juvenal's sixth *Satire*, for example, gains from being read as an exercise (*progymnasma*), specifically, an exaggerated example of the abstract question (*thesis*), 'Ought a man to marry?', which was a standard exercise given to Roman schoolboys. Similarly, *Satire* 12 is a satiric version of the speech of welcome (*prosphonetikon*); and *Satire* 3 is illuminated by being read as a (satiric) version of the farewell speech of the departing traveller (*syntaktikon*), combined with the school essay on the topic 'Is town or country life better?' (Quintilian *Institutio Oratoria* 2.4.24). *Satire* 5 can be seen as a dissuasion from the life of a parasite, with its opening and closing addresses to the servile client Trebius. *Satires* 1 and 2 perhaps have more in common with forensic than declamatory oratory, in their presentation respectively as the self-defence of the satirist and invective on the theme of deviant sexuality (which featured prominently in legal speeches). The fact that Juvenal's audience of élite men had all shared in experience of the declamation schools makes it likely that they would have understood immediately Juvenal's rhetorical framework and would have appreciated the divergences from that framework introduced for satirical purposes.

One of the most prominent features of the declamatory education was the presentation of material in terms of role models. Conduct was frequently described in terms of *exempla*, both positive and negative, for protreptic* and apotreptic* purposes (i.e. to 'turn' the listener 'to' and 'from' a particular course of action). Quintilian discusses the use of *exempla*, which he regards as a kind of proof, at *Institutio Oratoria* 5.11. Even more useful is the handbook of such *exempla* which survives from antiquity in the *Facta et Dicta Memorabilia* ('Deeds and Sayings Worthy of Record') of Valerius Maximus, writing under Tiberius. This is a collection of 967 stories about named individuals taken from various authors and organised into categories to illustrate various characteristics,

e.g. on the rise from humble origins and the decadence of the nobility
(3.4 and 3.5, cf. Juvenal *Satire* 8), on *pietas* ('duty', 5.4-6) and on
anger (9.3). The difference between oratory and satire is, not surpris-
ingly, that in satire apotreptic *exempla*, the extremes of bad conduct,
predominate. Juvenal's *Satires* are teeming with negative *exempla*;
the fewer positive *exempla* function as a foil (e.g. towards the close
of *Satire* 2 where Juvenal uses characters from the Republican era as
exempla of pristine virtue). *Satire* 1 is a striking case of the phenomenon of exemplarity on a larger scale: the catalogue of the
wicked people who populate Rome presents an inversion of a parade
of the finest and most glorious *exempla*, such as the parade of
Aeneas' descendants in Virgil *Aeneid* 6.756-853.

Another element of the training in declamation was the use of *loci
communes*, literally 'commonplaces', stock themes which might usefully
be inserted in a variety of contexts. The elder Seneca (?55 BC - ?AD 40)
lists four chief types of commonplaces as (1) changes in luck (*de
fortuna*), (2) human cruelty and pity (*de crudelitate*), (3) contemporary
decadence and praise of former times (*de saeculo*), and (4) the advantages and inconveniences of wealth (*de diuitiis*) (*Contr.* 1 pref. 23).
To these can be added the *loci philosophumeni* (*Contr.* 1.7.17) on
conscience, remorse, true nobility and similar ideas. Two manifestations
of the *locus de saeculo* will suffice by way of illustration. In the first the
specific theme is gluttony:

> The master will eat a mullet dispatched from Corsica, or from
> Tauromenium's rocks, now that our local waters
> are all fished out and exhausted. Gluttony's on the rampage;
> the nearest grounds have been swept clean by the market's
> non-stop
> trawling. Tyrrhenian fish are not allowed to grow up.
>
> (Juvenal 5.92-6)

In the second the specific theme is morality, as women ancient and
modern are compared. Stone Age woman is praised:

> She wasn't at all like Cynthia, or like that other lady
> whose lustrous eyes were dimmed and spoiled by the death of
> a sparrow.
> Giving her breasts, with plenty to drink, to her mighty babes,
> she was often more uncouth than her acorn-belching husband.
> People, of course, lived differently then, when the world was young

and the sky was new – people born from the riven oak
or freshly fashioned from mud, who had no proper parents.
Some, if not many, traces of Chastity's former presence
may have survived under Jove, before the Lord of Olympus
had yet acquired a beard, before the Greeks were ready
to swear on another's life, when fruits and cabbages flourished
untroubled by thieves, and no one bothered with garden walls.

(Juvenal 6.7-18)

Satire and epic

I have suggested that Roman satire shares some of its frameworks and features with standard rhetorical exercises and formats which would have been familiar to the entire élite audience. The rhetorical element is not the only influence of this kind. Roman satire continually exhibits a close familiarity with other literary genres and works, above all, the epic poems which formed the basis of the Roman education curriculum. This relationship of intertextuality* emerges both in brief allusions to incidents in Homer and Virgil and in the appropriation of epic frameworks for parts of poems and entire poems. There are also cases of parody and, in at least one case (*Satire* 4, see p.49), sustained parody of a lost but identifiable epic poem. It is satire's use of the metre of epic, the hexameter, which continually and inevitably invites comparison with the elevated subject-matter and tone of epic poetry and reminds us of satire's propensity to debase and debunk epic material. A few examples will show the importance of this phenomenon for the appreciation of the intellectual and entertaining side of satire, even at moments when it is masquerading as highly realistic.

The closing words of Horace's satire about the pest (*Sat.* 1.9.78) are a quotation (in Latin translation) from Homer *Iliad* 20.443: 'Thus was I saved by Apollo.' In Homer Apollo saves Hector from a duel with Achilles; in Horace the quotation is applied to the bathetic* (lowly) context of Horace's preservation from the pest who is whisked away into court, under the nose of the statue of Apollo. In *Satire* 3, Juvenal includes similarly bathetic mock-epic detail in the incident in which a man is killed in a traffic accident and ends up sitting on the banks of the Styx while his household makes preparations for his return home, oblivious of his demise (3.257-67). Phrases which recall Virgil's description of the Underworld in *Aeneid* 6 are juxtaposed with words and ideas from a different register (for discussion see 'City and Country' 35, in my *Satire and Society in Ancient Rome*). A few lines later, in the encounter between the unfortunate man on his way home from a dinner-party and a mugger, Juvenal reworks the portrayal of Achilles' restlessness caused by his grief at Patroclus' death (Homer *Iliad* 24.10-11) to emphasise how utterly unheroic the drunken thug is:

> Your drunken thug who has failed, by chance, to record a
>   murder
> pays the price; he spends the night as Achilles did
> when mourning his friend; he lies on his face and then on his
>   back.
> For sleep a brawl is needed.

(3.278-82)

These two examples are brief and limited cases of specific allusion. Sometimes the epic reference provides a more extended framework, either general or specific. Horace introduces his narrative of the contest in insults between the two rustic buffoons in *Satires* 1.5 in a classic epic mode, complete with invocation of the Muse, designed to underline the gulf between epic warriors and the combatants in this duel:

> Now, Muse, I pray,
> recount for me briefly the battle of Sarmentus the clown
> and Messius Cicirrus, and the lineage of the two contestants
> in the case. Messius was of glorious ancestry – the Oscans!
> Sarmentus' lady owner is still alive. With pedigrees like that
> they came to do battle.

(I.5.51-6)

More specific is Horace *Satires* 2.5 where a scene from *Odyssey* 11 provides the starting-point for the entire poem. Horace imagines an addition to Homer's scene in the Underworld in which Odysseus consults the prophet Tiresias:

> 'One more question, Tiresias, besides what you've told me.
> Tell me, what ways and means can I use to recover the wealth
> I've lost?...Why are you laughing?'

(2.5.1-3)

Horace's updated, humorous version of Tiresias proceeds to advise Ulysses/Odysseus to make money by ingratiating himself with elderly rich men: the poem consists of a lecture based entirely on how to succeed at legacy-hunting.

A still more specific and detailed relationship with epic occurs in Juvenal *Satire* 4. Most of this poem consists of an epic-style narrative, introduced by an epic-style invocation of the Muses:

> Begin, Calliope – and do sit down, it isn't a matter
> for singing; the theme is a true event; recount it, ye maidens
> of Pieria – and may I win some credit for calling you maidens.
>
> (4.34-6)

The narrative which follows describes how Domitian summons his cabinet of advisers to advise him what to do with an enormous fish which has been presented to him, because there is no dish big enough to hold it. There follows a catalogue of Domitian's eleven advisers and then a narrative of the advice they give. With the decision to make a dish big enough, the advisers are dismissed.

There is sufficient evidence to suggest that Juvenal is debunking a specific epic poem, now lost to us, Statius' *De Bello Germanico* ('On the German War', written under the emperor Domitian, AD 81-96). The only fragment which survives is quoted by a scholiast (i.e. an ancient commentator) on Juvenal. It is part of a catalogue of advisers which names three of the men who feature in *Satire* 4. This can be no coincidence. It is almost certain that Statius' poem praised the emperor Domitian for his campaigns in Europe, given Statius' other panegyrical writings. In the lost epic, the emperor's advisers were presumably summoned for serious debate on a matter of military urgency and given heroic treatment by Statius. In *Satire* 4 Juvenal substitutes the trivial matter of the fish, thus denigrating Domitian's military achievements and perhaps Statius' panegyrical style too. This example shows vividly how satirical discourse can be shaped by factors such as intertextuality with a recent epic poem – and how this can happen at the very moment when the satirist is claiming truth for his narrative. In the quotation above, the satirist introduces his narrative by claiming that his 'theme is a true event'. Again, we need to remember that satire is a dramatic form and that the satirist's first aim is persuade his audience and not to give a realistic account of Roman life.

Using satire as evidence

And yet it *is* possible to use the texts of Roman satire for some degree of illumination of Roman culture. Satire cannot necessarily be used to provide hard 'facts' or data (if such ever exist) about specific practices, since these details may be exaggerated or exceptional in some way. But it can draw attention to areas of social and cultural concern. The Russian Formalist movement in the first few decades of the twentieth century expressed the view that the essence and the value of poetry was the way in which it could 'make strange' the familiar. This works well enough for satire, both ancient and modern. Satire invites us to take another look at aspects of people's behaviour that we take for granted or have become inured to. It highlights issues about which society is or ought to be concerned.

Two examples will illustrate this point. Juvenal devotes his entire second book, which consists of the gigantic *Satire* 6, to the theme of Roman marriage. This might be thought to be an indication that the institution of marriage was in a terrible state. But the problems involved in trying to deduce anything concrete about the behaviour of Roman wives and husbands are enormous, not least because of Juvenal's creation of a raging misogynist to deliver this dissuasion from marriage. What the poem does suggest, however, is that Roman marriage was an area of anxiety which formed a legitimate focus for an entertaining *tour de force* of this kind. And if we set this poem alongside other kinds of evidence, such as the evidence of inscriptions, we find a substantial coherence in terms of the general concerns (as opposed to specific allegations). Roman epitaphs for wives, for example, exhibit the same sort of concerns about fidelity and chastity that run through *Satire* 6. In the inscriptions, a woman is particularly praised if she dies *univira*, that is, having had only one husband. The same concern emerges, but with satirical presentation, in the voice of Juvenal's angry misogynist:

> Thus she rules her man; but soon she resigns her dominion
> and passes through a succession of homes, with her veil in
>   tatters,
> and then flies back, refilling the dinge in the bed she deserted.
> The doors so recently decked, the house with its coloured
>   awnings,
> and the boughs still fresh and green on the threshold – all are
>   abandoned.
> And so the tally grows: that makes eight husbands exactly
> in five Octobers, a feat which should be carved on her tombstone.
>
> (6.224-30)

Satire 6 is not and should not be read as an objective account of Roman women's behaviour. A poem like this reveals more about Roman men's fears and prejudices about women than about women themselves – and it makes entertainment out of those fears.

The same is true of the phenomenon central to Roman satire and to Roman society – *amicitia*, 'friendship', the relationship between *amici*, that is, patrons and clients. Juvenal's picture is one of a complete break-down in that relationship. The topic is treated graphically throughout Book 1, culminating in *Satire* 5, the poem which portrays the alienation of patron from client in terms of food. Virro, the patron, has invited his humble client Trebius to dinner at the last minute, so there are no empty places, and serves up two menus, one consisting of fine food for himself and guests of like status, the other consisting of inferior food – or, at some stages of the meal, no food at all – for guests such as Trebius. This is not a novel theme in Roman literature: there are similar criticisms of the unequal feast in Martial and Pliny (*Letters* 2.6). And, doubtless, unequal feasts did happen. But Juvenal has taken the raw material and served up an elaborate and exaggerated version of this theme. In so doing, he is not interested in recording abuses of the *amicitia* relationship so much as drawing attention to an area of Roman life laden with anxieties. The poem is not simply an attack on the patron's shoddy and uncivilised treatment of his lowly client. It is also a *suasoria* directed at the client, a dissuasion from the degrading life-style of the parasite which renders him a hired buffoon or a slave. Patron and client corrupt one another so that their relationship turns into that of master and slave. That is, the poem itself depicts an entertainingly extreme version of the unequal feast; but the fact that this topic merits such extravagant attention is a reflection of the importance of *amicitia* in Roman society. It suggests that there are profound anxieties about that relationship both for the individual and for society as a whole.

In short, if we simply accept the view argued by the satirist, we shall get only a partial and limited picture. But if we are prepared to take a larger view – to admit a more complex picture – then we can gain some perspective on which issues are important for the Roman élite who make up the authors and audience of these poems. And this more complex picture is likely to be much more accurate than the simplistic black-and-white views peddled by a satirist who is created for entertaining effect by his author. The authority of the satirist is an element of the dramatic creation designed to sustain the impression of accuracy and moral seriousness. We do, however, have the choice of challenging the authority of the satirist. And it is in the process of doing this that satire can be made to yield illumination of central concerns in Roman society.

Chapter 7
Satirists and Audiences

Voices and victims, authors and audiences

The particular dramatic form of satire is what the Romans call *sermo*, which may be translated as 'conversation', 'chat' or 'dialogue'. Lucilius and Horace both use this word to denote their compositions. This tells us something important about the genre of satire: it is a form which acknowledges the presence of some kind of audience and which invites a response from that audience. In this final chapter, then, I want to look at Roman satire in terms of the relationships involved between the different parties, internal and external: the author and audience outside the text, and the voices, victims, addressees and audiences inside the text. The relationship between the author and the mask or voice he creates has been covered above in Chapter 1. There remain the relationships between the voice and its victims, between the voice and the addressee(s) named within the poems and between the voice and any audience implied within the poem. And finally there is the relationship between the voice and the audience outside the poem (i.e. us, potentially) – which is the relationship with which most scholarship on satire has been concerned.

Satire most simply and most obviously operates by attacking individuals or groups marked out as different and deviant. Attacks on such groups tend to create solidarity between the active and passive participants in the performance of satire, that is, between the voice and his (assumed) audience, which may be an assumed internal audience (for example, Horace appealing to the élite group of Maecenas or in Juvenal Umbricius' certainty that all decent Roman citizens will agree with his complaints) or an assumed external audience consisting of the original live audience at the first performance/reading of the poem and subsequent audiences and readers.

But satire is not always that simple. Sometimes the object of attack is the addressee within the poem, sometimes it is the audience listening to the performance of the satire and sometimes it is even the voice himself who is the victim. Analysing this complex web of relationships will enable us to see more clearly some of the dynamics of satire, in particular how the poet wields his poetic powers by using the different voices he creates to push us towards a particular reaction. Awareness of these dynamics should, in turn, help us to be more responsive, subtle and independent readers of satire. A further complicating factor is that these relationships vary subtly according to the different forms of presentation chosen by the author – monologue, dialogue, and letter. I shall use this division to structure my discussion.

Monologue

The dramatic monologue is the commonest form used in Roman verse satire. Unlike the monologues (usually soliloquies*) of characters in drama, which tend to be of a deliberative mode, weighing the merits of different courses of action, the monologues of satire usually assume the existence of addressee(s) and/or an audience. They are (more or less) self-conscious performances.

The satiric monologue is an extremely versatile form. Three broad categories leap to mind, although there are doubtless others too. Firstly, there are sermon-type monologues, which are obviously indebted to the Greek tradition of the diatribe* (i.e. popular philosophy), often addressed to the world at large, the world passing by the street corner where the satirist has set up his soap-box. The opening three poems of Horace's first book of *Satires*, labelled the 'diatribes of Horace' by Niall Rudd (*The Satires of Horace* p. 1), conform to this model, as does the prologue to Persius' book of satires and the first *Satire* of Juvenal. Another obvious case is Juvenal's *Satire* 10 (discussed in Chapter 3), on the foolish objects of prayers, with its clear structure introducing each new topic in an ordered way.

Secondly, there are persuasions (*suasoriae*) addressed to specific individuals, usually named, urging them towards or (more often in satire) deterring them from a particular course of action or outlook (that is, protreptic and apotreptic arguments). There are numerous examples in Juvenal. *Satire* 6 is a dissuasion from marriage addressed to Postumus, a bachelor who has decided to take the plunge into family life. *Satire* 5 is a dissuasion from the life of a parasitic client addressed directly to Trebius who submits himself to humiliations again and again. Umbricius' tirade in *Satire* 3 is a condemnation of city life, addressed initially at least to his friend, and *Satire* 8 is a persuasion to good conduct addressed to Ponticus, a man with a name which suggests he relies for his status on the successes of his ancestors rather than on his own excellent behaviour. Persius' *Satire* 4 is another example, where the poem opens with Socrates addressing his most celebrated 'historical' pupil, Alcibiades.

Thirdly, there are narratives. Horace includes two 'autobiographical' narratives in his first book, *Satires* 1.5 and 1.9, together with the narrative delivered by the wooden statue of Priapus in *Satires* 1.8. Narratives are rarer in Juvenal, though the mock-epic sections of *Satires* 4 and 12 represent this element. These three categories all have fairly obvious analogues in classical dramatic works, with the third type, narratives, perhaps most closely resembling messenger speeches, from which the remaining characters and the audience must draw the moral for themselves.

The overriding dynamic of the satiric monologue is that of the satirist attacking his victims. The victims divide between 'out-groups' (to use Amy Richlin's term, 'Invective against women in Roman satire' *Arethusa* 17 (1984) p. 67) and the extremely powerful. 'Out-groups' are categories of powerless people, easily identifiable and reduced to stereotypes, such as foreigners (Juvenal 3), effeminates (Juvenal 2), women (Juvenal 6) and so on. The addressee and/or implied audience are assumed to be in agreement with the satirist in picking on these people as victims. On this view, satire can perhaps be seen as a form of scape-goating, driving out the 'other' element from society, closing ranks, reinforcing the status quo, much on the lines of Elliott's analysis (see Chapter 5). Attacks on the other kind of victim, the rich and powerful, show the same normalising aim. The rich and powerful are attacked when they break the rules, for example, the rules about civilised conduct towards their humble clients (Juvenal 5) or their courtiers (Juvenal 4). Again, the satirist presumes the agreement of his audience. A central strand throughout is the commendation, implicit or explicit, of a narrow range of acceptable behaviour; all deviations are pounced upon.

This dynamic tends to carry the reader along with the satirist's perspective and reinforces the authority of the satirist figure (discussed in Chapter 6). This probably accounts for the tendency towards biographical readings of satire, the predominant mode of interpretation in the early twentieth century. But if we are alert, there may be other reactions available. Take Swift's *A Modest Proposal* (published 1729), a typical example of the satiric seduction of an audience. The speaker in this essay outlines the Irish problem and urges that a solution is required. He seems eminently reasonable – until we realise the solution he is proposing. His solution is to eat the babies of Irish poor. This monstrous proposal makes us dissent at this point. So too with Roman satire. Umbricius' condemnation of city life in *Satire* 3 is obviously one-sided. So too is the tirade against Roman wives in *Satire* 6. These monologues then contain possibilities for satire directed against the satirist too, as well as against the ostensible victims.

Consider for a moment Horace's treatment of *amicitia*, so markedly different from Juvenal's (discussed in Chapter 6). Most of the material relating to *amicitia* in Horace's satirical writings is concerned with the élite group around Maecenas, particularly with the standards by which the group judges itself and others. If we are persuaded by Horace's satirist, the standards of that group are the last word. If, on the other hand, we allow a dissenting voice, we can see that there are different ways of looking at standards. In Horace's narrative of the 'Journey to Brindisi' (1.5, discussed in Chapter 3) we might laugh at the vulgar slanging match between the two rustic buffoons and at the 'fussy host' who nearly burns down his own house – or we might find the supercilious and patronising attitude of Maecenas' clique obnoxious. Similarly, in Horace's complaint about the pest (1.9, discussed in Chapter 4), we might ruefully sympathise with his plight and his desperation to get away from the dreadful social climber – or we might reflect that Horace himself was in the same position of wanting to be accepted by Maecenas' group only a few poems earlier (e.g. 1.6). These monologues attempt to determine our reaction to the satirist as favourable. Yet it remains possible to read them in another way which also admits criticism of the satirist. This criticism might even extend to our criticism of ourselves, ultimately, if we catch ourselves being taken in by the satirist's persuasion, then adjust our reaction when we realise that we are assenting to an opinion which conflicts with our basic attitudes and beliefs. This is the phenomenon which Persius so accurately describes in Horace (a passage quoted previously, at the beginning of Chapter 4):

> The rascal Flaccus touches every fault in his friend while
> he laughs and, once he's got in, he frolics around his heart,
> clever at hanging the public from his cleared nose.
>
> (1.116-18)

The satiric monologue, then, is a more complex form than may appear at first. Although the satirist may assume that he is addressing a sympathetic audience, the author may invite the audience to condemn his satirist for his one-sided views, as we have just seen. Another complication is that the audience may identify with the victims. This (obviously) depends on the individuals in the audience: do we recognise ourselves in the victims pilloried in satire? To do so is obviously uncomfortable and something we might resist. But it probably helps to explain the very wide range of reactions to satire: if we feel vulnerable we are more likely to be offended and hostile to the satirist. Or, if we suppress our awareness of our vulnerability, we may energetically endorse the satirist's attacks on his victims. In short, there are likely to be as many reactions to a performance of satire as there are members of the audience at that performance. Monologue is the satiric form which engenders the closest engagement between satirist and audience.

Dialogue

In contrast with monologue, which draws in the audience with its tendency to seduce them into adopting the satirist's perspective, dialogue shuts out the audience. In a true dialogue, we the audience are rendered eavesdroppers to a conversation between the satirist and his interlocutor. One consequence of this is that our presence is not acknowledged – the satirist is not ostensibly performing for us – and we can therefore relax into observation of the relationship between the two characters involved in the conversation. But this is not to say that we the audience are not subject to manipulation!

There are two broad categories of dialogue in Roman satire. The first is where we are invited to sympathise with one interlocutor and to dislike the other. This pattern occurs particularly where a sermoniser appears and delivers a lecture to the other character, who is in effect his victim, compelled to remain in his seat listening until the other has finished. Horace explores this model in several poems in his second book of *Satires*. In 2.3 and 2.7 Horace is subjected to second-hand recitations of hard-line Stoic sermons from an ex-auctioneer and his own slave Davus, respectively. And in 2.4 (discussed in Chapter 4) Catius repeats to him a lecture on gastronomy which elevates food to the level of the highest good. Persius 3 is another poem which uses the same model, again presenting a severe Stoic line to an amiable listener. In these cases, the lecturer or sermoniser is portrayed as rude or intolerant, unpleasant or cranky. He exposes his own foolish obsession by the content and/or length of his sermon. This in effect guarantees the audience's sympathy for the sermoniser's victim, whether or not the victim's innocence or humility is emphasised.

The second broad category of dialogue is where we dislike both parties pretty much equally. The author achieves this by having them both reveal themselves as unpleasant individuals. Horace 2.5 is a satiric version of the Homeric episode in which Odysseus (here Ulysses) consults the prophet Tiresias in the underworld. In Horace's poem, the two characters could hardly be further removed from their originals. In reply to Ulysses' question about how best to recover the property he has lost, Tiresias is depicted advising him to become a legacy-hunter, that is, to prey on rich and childless men and women in the hope of being named in their wills. And Ulysses is no better than Tiresias: he accepts this cynical advice. Another example is Juvenal's only experiment in sustained dialogue, *Satire* 9. This is a conversation between an unnamed speaker and Naevolus, a client who has been rejected by his patron after satisfying his patron's own sexual needs and after fathering children for him and who is now angrily ranting about the ungrateful patron. Naevolus is self-evidently an unpleasant character – his lack of moral scruples, his greed and his snideness in complaining about the patron behind his back all ensure our low opinion of him. But the unnamed speaker in whom he confides is equally unpleasant. He leads Naevolus on with a false appearance of sympathy and entices him into more and more indiscretions about his former patron, while making ironical remarks (the irony is lost on Naevolus) that reveal his own strong sense of superiority to Naevolus.

Perhaps the central difference between the monologue form and the dialogue form is that whereas the monologue tends to draw in the audience and provide a ready-made reaction for them (whether or not that reaction is, ultimately, accepted), the dialogue keeps the audience at arms' length and provides it with no built-in interpretation. The audience has to decide which of the two speakers, if any, is in the right and deserves its sympathy. Interpreting dialogue is hard work.

Letter

The last form to be considered is the satiric verse letter (to be distinguished from the prose letters of Cicero, Seneca and Pliny, and from other verse letters such as Ovid's). This form was used by Lucilius and developed by Horace, in *Epistles* 1, which consists of 20 'letters', and in the longer poems, the letter to Augustus (*Ep.* 2.1), the letter to Florus (*Ep.* 2.2) and the so-called *Ars poetica*, addressed to the Pisones. The letter form is closely related to the dialogue form. In both, the audience is in the same situation of being eavesdroppers. This is because the letter is (fictionally) part of an ongoing correspondence – a dialogue in writing, in effect. It represents the words of one party responding to the words of the other party as (so the pretence goes) expressed in a letter received from that person. In effect, it represents just one side of a dialogue.

The effect of this is to make the satire very oblique and indirect. The satirist, now transformed into a correspondent, has an addressee, who may or may not be his victim. The author directs the sympathy of us, the audience, through his satirist's attitude to his addressee – polite, humble, bold, patronising, friendly. Most of these attitudes are found in Horace *Epistles* 1: he is polite to his patron Maecenas (1.1, 7 and 19), friendly to Albius (1.4) and to Aristius Fuscus (1.10) and rather patronising to his estate-manager, a slave (1.14). And the audience is left free to identify with the situation of any of the characters, as it wishes.

The letter form is perhaps the hardest to sustain. Its tendency is to revert towards the monologue form. Persius *Satire* 6 is a good example. It starts as a friendly letter to Caesius Bassus who is spending the winter at the coast but develops into a hostile monologue addressed to his heir, who, he imagines, is putting him under pressure to be more careful with money. The transition is achieved through the theme of living a pleasant life of independence and self-sufficiency: this is evidently the model exemplified by Bassus and aspired to by the satirist – and under threat from the heir. This phenomenon of epistle turning into monologue is even clearer in Horace's long letters on literary matters: the largely didactic tone and teacherly mask adopted by Horace tend to obscure the epistolary form.

Interpreting the drama of satire

Even the different forms available to the author of satire prove slippery, in the end. Monologue, dialogue, letter: all are first and foremost dramatic forms. And in this special type of drama the relationships between the different parties – authors and audiences, voices and victims – can take on many different configurations.

I shall finish with a passage from Roman satire which has been popular through the ages – and which illustrates graphically some of the difficulties of interpreting satire. It is the story of the town mouse and the country mouse in Horace *Satires* 2.6. This fable is at the same time possibly the most immediate and appealing story in the whole of extant Roman satire and, paradoxically, one of the most difficult passages to interpret. (For an excellent, if traditional, literary critique of the fable see D. West 'Of Mice and Men: Horace *Satires*, 2.6.77-117' in *Quality and Pleasure in Latin Poetry* ed. T. Woodman and D. West, Cambridge, 1974, pp.67-80.) Its surface simplicity is in conflict with its narrative complexity: it occurs in Horace's narrative of pleasant social occasions at which another person retells an old fable of Aesop:

Among all this, our neighbour Cervius babbles away with his
  old wives'
tales that suit the case. If anyone praises Arellius' wealth,
unaware of its anxieties, he begins like this: Once upon a time,
they say, a country mouse welcomed to his humble hole
a city mouse...

(Sat. 2.6.77-81)

And the remainder of the satire is devoted to the telling of the fable, with
no return to any wider framework at the end. It seems as if the moral of
the fable – that a simple, safe and independent life is preferable to a
luxurious and dangerous life of dependency – is designed to stand as the
moral for the satire as a whole. But, we might ask, who is actually
responsible for the telling of this fable – and, by extension, endorsing its
moral? Horace the author? 'Horace' the character within the poem? The
neighbour Cervius? Or even Aesop? And which of the audiences is the
target of the fable? The original group of neighbours, including 'Horace',
at the dinner-party in the country? The implied audience in the poem as
a whole, that is those inside Maecenas' coterie and those outside who
envy those inside? Or the original Roman audience when Horace the poet
first produced this poem? Or any audience since then? Us?

This small example highlights the wide range of potential relationships between author and audience in the genre of satire. Satire is
always a tricky and slippery type of discourse to interpret. The author
tends to play games with us by creating a mask or voice, a satirist who
is persuasively and seductively authoritative, and then by undermining
that authority. This he does by writing into the mask some equivocation,
inconsistency or ambivalence which creates uncertainty for us about the
relationship between author and mask, between poet and *persona*. This
continual destabilisation can be very disconcerting. It suggests that there
are no final 'right answers', no 'correct' way of reading the texts of satire.
But if we realise that we are a part of the drama, that we are not just
passive agents listening to a monologue or dialogue, that we can take an
active role in responding to what we hear and interpreting it for ourselves,
this should and will help us to be more subtle and independent readers
of satire.

Suggestions for Further Study

1. What reasons are there for treating satire as performance?

2. Juvenal's satiric mask develops from passionate anger into detached mockery. What are the artistic advantages and disadvantages of these two masks?
   Passages for discussion: Juvenal 1.1-30, 10.346-366

3. What are the essential differences between the masks used by Horace in the first and second books of his satires?
   Passages for discussion: Horace *Satires* 1.5.77-85, 2.4.76-95

4. To what extent is the aggression of Roman satire an expression of masculinity?
   Passages for discussion: Horace *Satires* 1.8.37-50, Persius *Satire* 1.98-106, *Satire* 4.33-45, Juvenal 2.82-98, 2.117-136, *Satire* 6

5. How do the rhetorical strategies available to the smiling satirist differ from those available to the angry satirist?
   Passages for discussion: Horace *Satires* 1.1.13-42, Juvenal 1.87-116

6. Suggest how the idea of changing masks helps illuminate Horace's changing tone towards his patron Maecenas.
   Passages for discussion: Horace *Satires* 1.6.45-64, 2.6.40-58, *Epistles* 1.7.1-13

7. What do the victims of the anger in Juvenal *Satires* 1-6 have in common?
   Passages for discussion: Juvenal 1.22-80, 2.1-10, 3.58-85, 3.131-153, 4.144-154, 5.12-41, 6.634-661

8. How do we decide whether to regard the satirist as a dangerous criminal or brave citizen?
   Passages for discussion: Horace *Satires* 1.4.78-103, Persius *Satire* 1.107-134, Juvenal 1.158-171

9. Why do feasts play so prominent a part in Roman satire? What connection, if any, is there between food and friendship (*amicitia*)? To what extent do the hosts and the food fall into clearly defined categories?

Passages for discussion: Horace *Satires* 2.6.65-117; Juvenal 5.158-73

10. To what extent is the chatty style of Horace's satirist a cover for élitism?

Passages for discussion: Horace *Satires* 1.3.55-71, 1.4.63-78, 1.10.64-75

11. Why are satirists so frequently depicted in a city setting? Why do they praise life in the country? How realistic do you think the portrayals of city life and country life in satire are?

Passages for discussion: Horace *Satires* 1.9.1-13, 2.6.15-39, *Epistles* 1.10.12-25; Persius *Satire* 6.6-17, Juvenal 1.30-51, 2.65-78, 3.268-301, 10.36-48

12. To what extent do the unmasculine men in Juvenal *Satire* 2 and the women in Juvenal *Satire* 6 correspond to male fears and fantasies? Suggest ways in which these poems can and cannot be used to provide evidence about Roman culture.

Passages for discussion: Juvenal 2.149-170, 6.21-52, 161-171, 286-345, 634-661

13. Roman verse satire uses the first person monologue more than any other form. What artistic opportunities are made available to the author of satire by this choice?

Passages for discussion: Horace *Satires* 1.9.1-21; Juvenal 6.161-171

14. When the author reveals that his satirist is sexist or racist or homo-phobic or snobbish or stupid or ignorant or unreasonable, how does that affect the way in which we as the audience react?

15. What, if anything, does Roman satire have in common with contem-porary forms of satire (e.g. *Private Eye* and *Spitting Image*)?

Suggestions for Further Reading

Original sources in translation

Horace, *Satires and Epistles*, translated by Niall Rudd, revised 2nd edition (Penguin, 1987)

Persius, *Satires*, translated by Niall Rudd, revised 2nd edition (Penguin, 1987)

Juvenal *The Satires*, translated by Niall Rudd with introduction and notes by William Barr (Oxford World's Classics, 1992)

Lucilius, *Satires* (fragments), translated by E.H. Warmington (Loeb Classical Library, *Remains of Old Latin* vol. 3, 1979)

Modern works of literary criticism

Anderson, W.S. *Essays on Roman Satire* (Princeton 1982). This is a most useful collection of all of Anderson's articles on the writers of verse satire published over many years. Anderson was central in establishing the use of *personae* in Roman satire and the opening essay on this theme (pp. 3-10) is important. Among the very detailed analyses of particular poems,there are articles which offer stimulating readings of the major authors: 'The Roman Socrates: Horace and his Satires' (pp.13-49); 'Persius and the Rejection of Society' (pp.169-193); the very influential piece 'Studies in Book 1 of Juvenal' (pp.197-254); and, for those interested in Juvenal's later satires, 'The Programs of Juvenal's Later Books' (pp. 277-292). Finally, a perceptive analysis of anger in Juvenal is provided in pp. 293-314 of the longer essay entitled 'Anger in Juvenal and Seneca'.

Braund, S.H., *Roman Verse Satire* (*Greece & Rome* New Surveys in the Classics no.23, 1992). Following the usual pattern of these surveys, this provides an author-by-author analysis with full bibliography. The emphasis is upon literary criticism. The brief first and last chapters, on approaches to satire (pp. 1-5) and an overview of the genre (pp. 56-88), are designed to stimulate discussion and challenge some of the older views of Roman satire.

Braund, S.H., (ed.) *Satire and Society in Ancient Rome* (Exeter, 1989). This slim volume contains five essays exploring how satire can and cannot be used as a source for Roman social history, with a brief introduction on the use of the *persona* in Roman satire. The essays are on themes of prominence in Roman satire: friendship (R. Mayer), city and country (S.H. Braund), law (J.D. Cloud), food (N. Hudson) and women (J.G.W. Henderson).

Coffey, M., *Roman Satire* (2nd edn. Bristol 1989). A full literary history of the genre of Roman satire from its origins. There are detailed sections on the satires of Lucilius, Horace, Persius and Juvenal and the final part is devoted to Menippean satire (by Varro, Seneca and Petronius), not covered in this book, whose authors chose a form consisting of prose and verse for their satire.

De Decker, J., *Juvenalis declamans* (Ghent, 1913). This monograph (in French) shows in great detail how Juvenal's *Satires* are shaped by declamatory rhetoric. It is a useful work of reference in which the significant themes of the schools of declamation treated by Juvenal are catalogued.

Elliott, R.C., *The Power of Satire: Magic, Ritual, Art* (Princeton, 1960). Chapter 1 is fascinating reading. Here Elliott proposes a link between satire and magic, with examples from ancient Greece, Arabia and Ireland. In Chapter 3 he suggests how the sophisticated literary genre of Roman verse satire uses Archilochean threats metaphorically. Chapter 4 on 'the satirist satirized' will be of interest to anyone studying English literature with its examination of misanthropes and Chapter 6 offers reasons why society dislikes and distrusts satire.

Freudenburg, K., *The Walking Muse. Horace on the Theory of Satire* (Princeton, 1993). Chapter 1 presents an excellent articulation of *persona* theory which Freudenburg then applies to Horace *Satires* 1.1-4, where (he argues) Horace creates a cynic philosopher of homespun philosophy and rhetoric whom he undermines at the same time by making his dogmatism misplaced and his moralising inept. Freudenburg is especially clear on the links between satire and comedy, e.g. he sees the 'floppy shoe' which 'Horace' wears as a signal that *persona* is that of a bumpkin or buffoon of comedy.

Kenney, E.J., 'Juvenal: Satirist or Rhetorician?' *Latomus* 22 (1963) 704-20. A fundamental article on Juvenal, arguing that the rhetoric of the declamatory schools is Juvenal's idiom.

Kernan, A., *The Cankered Muse: Satire of the English Renaissance* (New Haven, 1959). This book offers fascinating insights into English satire and shows a good awareness of the influence of Roman satire on later developments in the genre.

Richlin, A., *The Garden of Priapus. Sexuality and Aggression in Roman Humor* (revised edn. New York and Oxford, 1992). Richlin applies approaches drawn from psychology and anthropology to analyse the concept of obscenity in Roman society in general and in satire in particular. The chapter on sexual satire (pp. 164-209) is that most obviously relevant to readers of this book but the opening chapter on Roman concepts of obscenity (pp. 1-31) is also well worth reading: it tackles with clarity and learning a difficult issue in an area laden with culture-specific assumptions, for example which words are and are not 'four-letter words'.

Richlin, A., 'Invective against women in Roman satire' *Arethusa* 17 (1984) 67-80. This stimulating article examines the way in which women are attacked in Roman satire, from a feminist perspective. Very useful is Richlin's term 'out-groups' to denote (some of) the victims in satire: powerless people who are reduced to stereotypes and treated as 'other'.

Rudd, N., *The Satires of Horace* (Bristol, 1982). Essential for anyone studying Horace's Satires in depth. This is a thorough and methodical book but unfortunately it covers only the Satires and not the Epistles.

Rudd, N., *Themes in Roman Satire* (London, 1986). A book which breaks away from the literary survey approach to Roman satire. Rudd's six chapters instead deal with central themes of the poems: aims and motives, freedom and authority, style and public, class and patronage, Greek and the Greeks, women and sex. Within each chapter, the material is organised author by author, so that it is easy to discover (for example) Rudd's views on Horace's treatment of the Greeks.

Scott, I.G., *The Grand Style in the Satires of Juvenal* (Northampton, Mass., 1927). In this study Scott shows how Juvenal has taken the grand style associated with epic and adapted it to satire to provide a suitable vehicle for indignation. Her detailed analysis makes this another important work of reference.

Glossary of Technical Terms

Items which appear in the glossary are marked * on their first appearance in the book

apostrophe (noun) Direct address to a person, god or object. Lit. 'turning aside' from the narrative.

apotreptic (adjective) A story or speech designed to dissuade the listener from a course of action.

apotropaic (adjective) A ritual or charm or chant designed to 'turn away' evil spirits.

bathetic (adjective) The effect is bathetic (from the noun *bathos*, 'depth') when a low or ludicrous word or idea suddenly intrudes into an elevated context.

declamation (noun) The rhetorical training for public speaking. It consisted of exercises practised in the declamation schools, *suasoriae* (persuasions) and *controversiae* (disputes).

diatribe (noun) Type of sermon associated with street philosophers such as the Cynics, with an easy and informal style, often including anecdotes, proverbs and fables.

enargeia (noun) Vivid description of a scenario. This is a rhetorical term for the technique of creating a picture in the listener's mind.

genre (noun) Type of work, usually with a distinctive metre, length and content. E.g. poems in the genre of epic are long poems in the hexameter metre about heroes.

hexameter (adjective and noun) Metre used in epic and satire, consisting of six feet with a set pattern in the last two feet. The basic rhythm is the dactyl (long-short-short).

iambic (adjective) Metre used for poems of abuse. The basic rhythm is short-long.

ideology (noun) A set of ideas which express and reflect the aspirations of the culture which produces them.

intertextuality (noun) A relationship between two texts, which may include allusion or overt reference by one to the other, in which the later text is framed as a response to the earlier text.

limping iambics (noun) Type of iambic metre in which there is a trochee (long-short) or spondee (long-long) in the final foot, disrupting the iambic rhythm.

peroration (noun) Closing climax to a speech.

post-romantic (adjective) Affected by ideas of romanticism such as the focus on the individual, an interest in emotion and mysticism and an emphasis upon (the appearance of) spontaneity in poetry.

protreptic (adjective) A story or speech designed to encourage the listener to a course of action.

soliloquy (noun) A speech (monologue) spoken by one character on their own as a private debate.

Index of Poems Discussed